PAULA NADELSTERN

SNOWFLAKES

& QUILTS

C&T PUBLISHING

Copyright © 2001 Paula Nadelstern

Editor: Candie Frankel
Technical Editor: Karyn Hoyt
Copyeditor: Carol Barrett
Design Director/Book Designer: Aliza Kahn Shalit
Cover Designer: Aliza Kahn Shalit
Production Assistant: Tim Manibusan
Production Coordinator: Diane Pedersen
Illustrator: Richard Sheppard © 2001 C&T Publishing, Inc.
Cover Image: *Kaleidoscopic XXII: Ice Crystals*
Quilt Photography: Karen Bell, New York City
Instructional photos: John Wooden, Philadelphia, PA
Photos on page 10: Courtesy of The Jericho Historical Society, Jericho, VT

Published by C&T Publishing, Inc., P.O. Box 1456, Lafayette, California 94549

Library of Congress Cataloging-in-Publication Data
Nadelstern, Paula.
  Snowflakes & quilts / Paula Nadelstern.
     p. ; cm.
Includes bibliographical references and index.
  ISBN 1-57120-155-6
  1. Patchwork—Patterns. 2. Patchwork quilts. 3. Snowflakes in art.
I. Title: Snowflakes and quilts. II. Title.
  TT835 .N35 2001
  746.46'041—dc21
                            00-011630

Printed in Hong Kong
10 9 8 7 6 5 4 3 2 1

TABLE OF CONTENTS

To Eric

Thank you for being my mensch

and to Ariel

Thank you for being the

kind of person I always

hoped you would be

ACKNOWLEDGMENTS

Although I do not always like to write, I always love to have written. This particular writing owes much to many, including:

W. A. Bentley, the Snowflake Man, whose intellectual curiosity and generous spirit left a legacy well tended by the Jericho Historical Society. Its archivist, Ray Miglionico, is another generous soul whose invaluable help included connecting me to Duncard Blanchard, a retired atmospheric scientist, who made sure my snowflake commentary was crystal clear.

Candie Frankel, Karyn Hoyt, and Aliza Kahn of C&T Publishing, for respecting my vision and providing discerning skills with good-natured patience. To put it another way, these are the guys who make me look good. Thanks also to Todd Hensley, Lynn Koolish, Trish Katz, Diane Pedersen, Barb Kuhn (you were right), Kris Yenche, Lisa Loura, Letty Perez, Rick Lejano, and John Pilcher, whose joint efforts wrap up a C&T package and make sure it has a long, healthy life in the real world.

Karen Bell and John Wooden, photographers extraordinaire, for their fine focus.

Selim Benardette, Esther Zielinski, Anna Fishkin, David Lochner, Janice Ervin, Jacqueline Ganey, Susan Neill, Carol DeSousa, and the rest of the Benartex staff. Their combined expertise translated my design sensibility into cloth that is a joy to piece into snowflakes.

The Manhattan Quilters Guild: Teresa Barkley, Karen Felicity Berkenfeld, Jeanne Lyons Butler, Judy Doenias, Susan Ball Faeder, Yvonne K.C. Forman, Randy Frost, Iris Gowen, Marilyn Henrion, Emiko Toda Loeb, Diana Goulston Robinson, Lauren Rosenblum, Carmel Roth, Diane Rode Schneck, Robin Schwalb, Sandra Sider, Arle Sklar-Weinstein, John Swiatek, and Ludmila Upsenskaya. Being part of this creative, talented group has honed my insights and stimulated my intellect. Thank you for letting me and my quilts mature along with you and yours.

The members of the Art Quilt Network/New York, whose collective genius constantly amazes and inspires me.

Mary Austin, Elizabeth Barton, Marty Bowne, Victoria Faoro, Rose Hughes, Linda Joy, Shirley Levine, Cheryl Little, Karen Perrine, Lois Podolny, Wendy Richardson, Deborah Schwartzman, Deb Tilley, Lorraine Torrence, and Mary Lou Weidman. Quiltmaking led me to these wise, witty women whom I often rely on to rescue me from foibles foisted by fate or fabric.

Dawn Hall of Cherrywood Fabric, Diane Smith of Pieces of Eight, Bernina of America, Inc., Clover Needlecraft, Inc., and Hobbs Bonded Fibers for their generosity.

The quilters who graciously opened their homes, the students who taught me the power of a conversation, and the readers who encouraged me to write again by letting me know *Kaleidoscopes & Quilts* was a good read. And, of course, the quilter who gave me her husband's blue and white shirt in class. You know who you are...does he?

My mother, Clara Lyman, who ran any errand in walking distance, and my mother-in-law, Eva Nadelstern, who resuscitated this household often with her culinary talents.

Rosie Steinberg, Harriet Goldman, and Cheryl King, my oldest friends who may not remember everything any more but remember how we got here.

And Cathy Rasmussen, whose friendship and encouragement I dearly miss.

Kaleidoscopic XI: Snowfall, 1993, 63½" x 60"

INTRODUCTION

For years, I've pored over snowflake photomicrographs as if they were moon-scapes and I'm the one responsible for a safe landing. As of this writing, I haven't found any evidence of teensy frostbitten aliens, but I have concocted some design guidelines I'm happy to share. They can't possibly be scientifically true, because we all know snowflakes aren't really made out of blue fabric, but they work for me.

Back in the crafty seventies, I left the meandering path that stopped at every needlework option and headed straight into quiltdom. My baggage was filled with limited technical skills, a penchant for combining colors, and a sense based on the then available literature that color-filled quilts were the telltale sign of an amateur. Hopefully, once I'd sewn my wild quilts, a maturation process would kick in and narrow my palette. Eventually I, too, would make quilts both simple and pure. I would make a blue and white quilt.

Behold my first blue and white quilt: a pastiche of at least fifty-three fabrics and thirty-five colors. Because, in spite of my intent, committing random acts of color is what I do best. My quilts combine the symmetry and surprise of a kaleidoscope with the techniques and materials of quiltmaking. Working in a single design genre has taught me to trust my instincts, value serendipity, and accept what I am good at. The longer I continue to stretch one idea, the simpler and purer the answers to my questions become. It's just the product that looks more and more complex.

I first got the idea for piecing a snowflake six years into my series of kaleido-scopic quilts. The snowflakes evolved from my work with kaleidoscopes but demanded a different design analysis. The oohs, aahs, and pattern requests directed at *Kaleidoscopic XI: Snowfall* as we traveled together on the lecture cir-cuit prompted this book. As an author, I faced a predicament: Do I tell you every-thing I know (including some simpler solutions I've figured out since *Kaleidoscopes & Quilts* was published in 1996), or do I write a watered-down ver-sion that's less verbose—and less than complete? Years ago, I was on a now defunct Lifetime TV craft show and the hostess, reading my introduction off the Q-cards, announced: "Are you a quiltophobic? Paula Nadelstern promises me that making kaleidoscope quilts is fun and easy!" My heart sank.

I'm opting for the tell-all version. I value the work, the creative process, and my audience too much. After all, I'm not going to get to sit next to you at your sewing machine and demonstrate what I left out because it seemed too tedious or involved to explain. Like a much appreciated trail of bread crumbs, those are precisely the details that will lead you out of a conundrum.

Kaleidoscopic XXII: Ice Crystals, 2000, 41" x 54"

My underlying assumption is that you've already made your first few quilts. In Part 1, I explain my drafting, template making, and machine-piecing techniques. Part 2 explores the common hexagonal pattern, the endless variety of structural details inherent in real snow crystals, and color and fabric guidelines to help make the translation. Part 3's Workbook integrates technique with design as it takes you through snowflake construction step by step.

As you read through the text and study the diagrams, keep in mind, there are no real rules. I made this up! But the only way I know to pass on my guidelines is to cloak them authoritatively in black and white terms. The elusive artistic elements that catapult craft beyond the ordinary are found somewhere in the shades of gray. Take what I say and make it fit your quilt persona.

Before you begin, I'd like to introduce you to Wilson Alwyn Bentley, the Snowflake Man. In 1885, at the age of nineteen, he became the first person to photomicrograph a snowflake. (Although I refer to these stellar forms of nature as snowflakes, they are actually snow crystals. Snow*flakes* are made up of many ice crystals that collide and stick together as they fall to earth. Purists and atmospheric scientists know the difference.)

Wilson A. Bentley, c. 1885

Bentley spent the next forty-seven years observing, writing, and photographing almost 6,000 snowflakes on his working farm in Jericho, Vermont. He is credited with the remarkable discovery, now common knowledge, that no two snowflakes are alike. At Bentley's request, his photomicrographs have been preserved and made available to "scientists seeking truth, the artist searching for patterns of graceful form, and all to whom the beautiful in Nature has a strong appeal." In the late 1920s, the U.S. Weather Bureau organized a fundraising drive to publish the best of the Bentley photomicrographs. Out of 3,500 images, 2,500 were compiled in the book *Snow Crystals*, published shortly after Bentley's death in 1931. In 2000, the Jericho Historical Society preserved over 1,000 of these historical images in a digital CD-ROM archive.

The Snowflake Man in 1917

This book owes much to the Snowflake Man's intellectual curiosity and generous spirit. The early twenty-first century romantic in me responds to the late nineteenth-century Romanticist in him. "When a snowflake melted," Bentley reflected, "that design was forever lost. Just that much beauty was gone, without leaving any record behind." In this moment of fleeting infinity, I glimpse a quality shared by kaleidoscopes and snowflakes.

As W. A. Bentley ascertained, every snow crystal that floats to earth is unique and equally compelling. Like a good quilt, a snowflake doesn't form instantly. It grows. It starts with a tiny nucleus and develops a geometric pattern of remarkable regularity around it, changing in form as it encounters differing atmospheric conditions and temperatures on its free-fall journey to earth. That's why, like a quilt, each snowflake has its own unique story. As Bentley put it, "Was ever life history written in more dainty hieroglyphics?"

PART 1
THE TECHNICAL SNOWFLAKE

IN THE BEGINNING

TOOLS OF THE TRADE

The truth is, I don't really sew very well. But I want it to look like I do. Fabricating this illusion means using reliable tools. Think of it as trying to start a fire by rubbing two sticks together. It becomes a whole lot easier if one of the sticks is a match.

Using the same tools consistently from the beginning of a project to the end is just plain common sense. So is making sure all of your measuring devices (including graph paper and template plastic) agree with each other. Otherwise, your carefully measured pieces still might not fit together. Here's what you'll need:

❄ *Graph paper* with an eight-to-the-inch grid and bold inch lines. I buy graph paper in 11" x 17" and 17" x 22" pads.

❄ Sheets of see-through *gridded template plastic*, also with an eight-to-the-inch grid and bold inch lines. The grid serves as a ruler. Usually four 8½" x 10¾" sheets come in a package. Do not purchase long sheets rolled and sold in a tube. You could flatten these under your mattress for a year and they'll curl right back into a roll as soon as they make their escape.

❄ A thin, beveled-edge *grid ruler*. These clear, see-through plastic rulers are marked with a ⅛" grid. I keep a 6" x 1" ruler next to me, a 12" x 2" close by, and an 18" x 2" within hailing distance. I like these thin rulers for drafting. Thicker ones made for use with rotary cutters cast shadows and don't allow a pen or pencil to get really, really close to the ruler's edge.

❄ *Pencils* and a *pencil sharpener* to keep the lead tips pointy. Lines don't only have length. They also have width. When you outline a shape, you increase its size by the width of the marking.

❄ *White chalk pencils* that can be sharpened to a fine point to mark dark fabric.

❄ Ample *erasers*.

❄ *Extra fine-point permanent markers*. A marker should leave a thin, visible line and glide smoothly without stretching the fabric. I don't want to waste time searching for a line once it's drawn or increase the size of a template or patch with a plump line. My favorite pen is the PILOT® Extra Fine Point Permanent Marker, SCA-UF.

❉ Two or three *protractors* in different sizes with notations for both whole and half degrees. Bigger is better since the numbers and marks are easier to read. (See page 16 before going on a protractor purchasing spree.)

❉ Two scissors: *fabric scissors* and *template/paper scissors*.

❉ Set-up for rotary cutting, including a *rotary cutter, ruler, and mat*. For trimming patches, I like to use the Brooklyn Revolver, a circular rotary mat mounted on a lazy Susan (see Sources).

❉ A *sewing machine* with a well-defined ¼" seam allowance guide. On some machines, the edge of the presser foot is exactly ¼" from the needle. I sew my quilts on an aging yet spry Singer Featherweight™ that has a ¼" mark etched on the throat plate. Other machines come with a magnetic or screw-on accessory to indicate sewing lines. If your machine has no markings at all, make your own with a piece of masking tape on the throat plate. Measure from the needle using the same ruler or graph paper grid you'll be using to draft the design. Check it a few hundred times. This is important. Compulsiveness now will result in well-behaved patches later.

❉ Good *lighting*. Without it, anticipate eyestrain and frustration, courtesy of a palette filled with dark fabrics.

❉ *Mirrors*. Two mirrors, hinged or held together at a 60° angle and placed on top of a fabric, can become a design tool for identifying potential mirror image reflections.

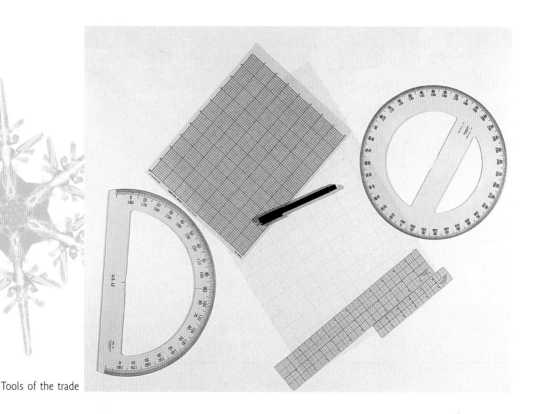

Tools of the trade

THE TRUTH ABOUT TRIANGLES

A snowflake is a hexagon. It is composed of six identical triangular wedges that radiate from a center point. When joined together, the six wedges equal 360°. This geometric tidbit is the key that enables six pieces of patchwork pie to fit together flawlessly. A snowflake's delicate pattern may be fashioned in ice, but the fact that its six wedges equal 360° is written in stone.

To calculate the angle of one of the wedges, you simply divide 360° by 6. The result, 60°, is the angle that must be at the apex, or tip-top, of each of the snowflake's six wedges.

But what if it isn't? What if, instead of 60°, you err on the generous side and one extra dainty degree slips past your protractor. Now, instead of 360°, you'll have 61° x 6, or 366°. Instead of a pleasingly flat center, a peaklike bulge erupts, ruining the view. Those extra 6° have to go somewhere and, sadly, this is not one of those mishaps you can press your way out of. Skimp on a measly degree (59° x 6 = 354°—need I say more?) and the snowflake collapses into an unsightly crater. In either case, you'll feel the overwhelming urge to appliqué something over the design's crucial center.

Now that we've established the importance of accurately drafting 60° at the apex of the triangle, it behooves us to understand one more jot of geometry. The triangle is not only 60° at the tip. The two legs, whether they measure 2" or 102", must maintain an accurate 60° angle along their entire length. If they don't, the hexagon won't lie flat when all six triangles are sewn together. The same 360° needed in the center for a graceful start is needed at the outer edges for an Esther Williams' style grand finale. Too many degrees and the perimeter wiggles where you were expecting nice and flat. Less than 360° and a ball starts to form.

There's no getting around it. The 60° triangle that you draft has got to be pretty perfect. It becomes the archetype, the original model from which all your other triangles will be derived. Whatever is done to the design once will be repeated six times. Every success, and every mistake, will be multiplied by six.

By the way, 60° makes for a plump roomy wedge. If you've had any previous experience with radial structures, you may be surprised by the expanse you get to fill up with fabric compared to more acute angles.

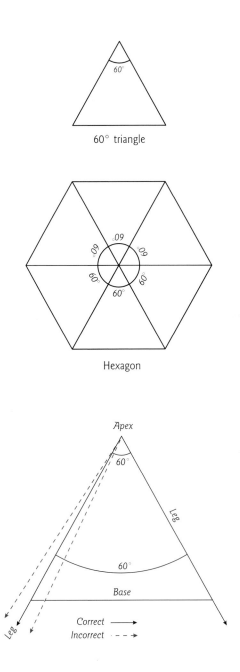

60° triangle

Hexagon

Apex

Leg

Leg

60°

60°

Base

Leg

Correct ⟶
Incorrect ┄⟶

HOW TO DRAFT A TRUSTWORTHY ANGLE
Establishing the Triangle's Center Axis

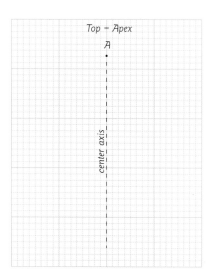

Top = Apex

A

center axis

The ⅛" grid on your graph paper will help you accurately draft a 60° triangle. Start by locating the bold vertical line that runs down the middle of the page. I designate this line the center axis; in geometric circles, it is called the axis of reflection or line of symmetry. Think of it as the backbone of your triangle. In the diagram, the center axis appears as a dotted line for easy identification. *Do not mark the center axis on your graph paper*. Only sewing lines will be marked inside the graph paper triangle. If you mark the center axis, you risk interpreting it as a sewing line later on.

Note that the top of the center axis, point A, is the apex of the triangle. It's really *really* important to situate point A at the intersection of the center axis and a bold horizontal line rather than arbitrarily at one of the ⅛" lines in between. This will allow you to maximize the graph paper's capacity to function like a ruler, a technique you will learn to rely on and appreciate.

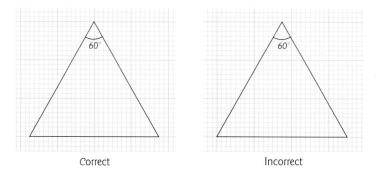

Correct   Incorrect

Using Protractors

Every protractor, no matter what its size, has three reference marks that must line up accurately with the graph paper grid. Locate the center reference mark at the middle of the straight edge (*a*), the 90° mark at the middle of the semi-circle (*b*), and the two 0° marks at either side (*c*). To use the protractor, lay it flat on the graph paper with the curved edge towards you. Align the center reference mark and the 90° mark on the center axis. Align the 0° marks on the bold horizontal line that passes through point A.

Here's the plan. Instead of measuring the entire 60° at once, we're going to do one half at a time by measuring 30° to the left of the center axis and the other 30° to the right. First, find the point on the graph

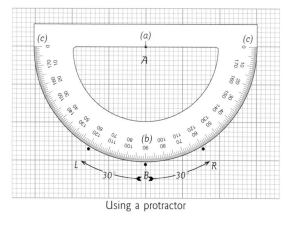

Using a protractor

paper where the 90° mark and the center axis coincide (point B). Count off 30° to the left of point B and establish point L by making a visible, but exquisitely delicate, pencil mark. Go back to point B, measure 30° to the right, and render point R with an equally anemic dot. Small, distinct markings are comprehensible and precise. Oversized, gloppy ones are beacons for inaccuracies waiting to wreak havoc. Note that you are not marking point B itself.

A line is a series of points. The more points that connect to make a line, the more accurate the line. Using one protractor provides two dots to connect for every line. Using a few protractors of different sizes results in multiple dots that vary in distance from the apex but still measure the identical angle. Connecting more than two dots ensures precision. Please note that these dots will not necessarily coincide with the graph paper's grid. Once you've made your dots, use a very sharp pencil and a straight edge to draft a line from point A through all the points L and another line from point A through all the points R.

Connecting multiple points

Using Tangents

What exactly are tangents? And why are we even talking about them? (For the record, I don't mean those mental digressions that all too frequently detour my attention.) For the mathematically challenged among us, don't panic. Count down five paragraphs until you reach The Chart. For the rest of you, here's the story behind How I Learned to Stop Worrying and Love the Tangent.

No matter how proficient I became with protractors, the problem of accurately extending the angle into long wedges remained. Experience taught me to double- and triple-check the accuracy of an angle when the success of a labor-intensive quilt rode on it.

The dictionary defines a tangent as a trigonometric function. Trigonometry is the study of the properties of triangles. My husband, the alternative high school principal, gets a kick out of saying that the only person he knows who uses her high school math is his wife, the quiltmaker. Please don't tell him I really don't deserve so much credit. What I realized is that the legs of a 60° triangle drafted accurately on eight-to-the-inch graph paper will land on the same grid points every time. If I could identify which grid points these were, I could use them to construct an accurate angle, or at least to check the accuracy of an angle made with a protractor.

At first I tried to identify these grid points using the semireliable eyeball method. This turned out to be not quite scientific enough for this occasion. Then I realized that the graph paper diagram provided information that could be put into an equation. For the next couple of years, I diddled with the equation for tangents but, truthfully, I was waiting for a mathematically savvy quilter to walk into my class, understand what I was babbling about, and solve my quandary through the knowledgeable use of computers. I always knew I could rely on the intelligence of quilters.

It is through the magic of computers and the skills of Susan Helzer of College Park, Maryland, and Susan Feldman of Kirkwood, Missouri, that I now present The Chart. ———➤

Plotting Points to Draft a 60° Angle

Vertical Length (along center axis)	Horizontal Length (to left and right of center axis)
2⅜"	1⅜"
3¼"	1⅞"
5⅝"	3¼"
6½"	3¾"
8⅞"	5⅛"
12⅛"	7"
14½"	8⅜"
15⅜"	8⅞"
17¾"	10¼"
21"	12⅛"
24¼"	14"

Remember when I said you'd be using the graph paper as a ruler? (Be honest. If the answer is no, go back to page 16.) If you plotted point A at the junction of two bold lines, the next part becomes easy. To use the chart, locate the first entry in the Vertical Length column (2⅜"). Beginning at point A, count down 2⅜" along the center axis. Resist the urge to mark a pencil dot. Instead, position a ruler horizontally on the 2⅜" grid line. Read across the chart to find the corresponding number in the Horizontal Length column (1⅜"). Starting from the center axis, and with the ruler still firmly planted on the 2⅜" horizontal line, count off 1⅜" to the left and make a visible but minuscule mark (point L). Go back to the center axis and repeat to the right (point R).

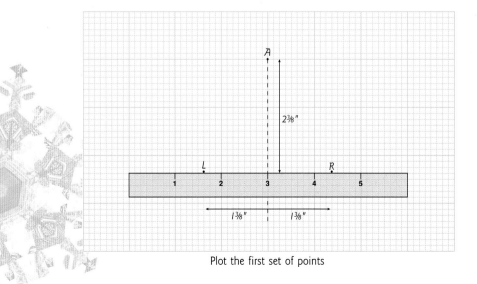

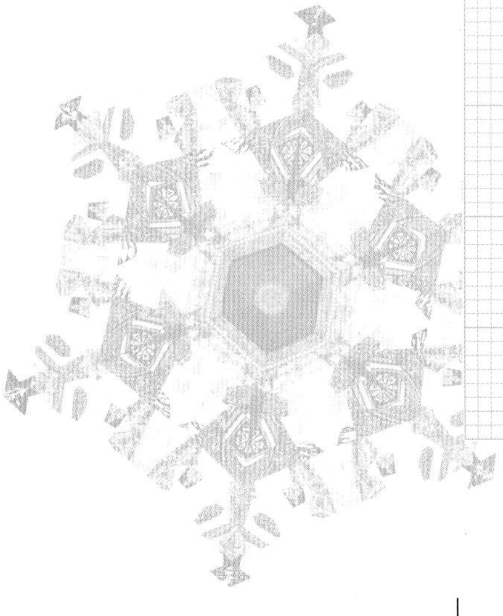

Plot the first set of points

Continue by moving the ruler down to the chart's next Vertical Length measurement (3¼"), read across the chart, and plot the corresponding left and right points.

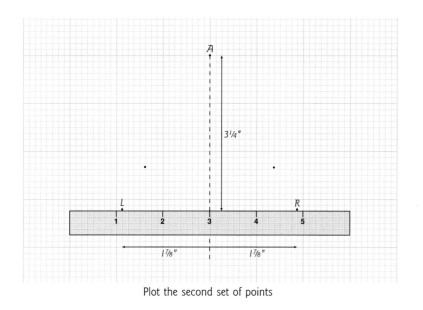

Plot the second set of points

Tip:

In case you're wondering, the reason why I don't mark the vertical length measurements on the graph paper is to keep the interior of the triangle clear. Once we move on to the design stage, markings made to draft the angle become confusing artifacts. We have new marks to make, new fabrics to measure. This requires a triangular tabula rasa, waiting spotless and pristine.

Repeat the process until you have marked three or more left and right dot positions. Connect the dots to the apex with a straight line and you will have an accurate 60° wedge.

THE VIEW FROM A HEXAGON

Hexagons behave differently from square quilt blocks. With the addition of four 30°-60°-90° triangles to fill out the corners, the final shape becomes a rectangle, not a square. The height of the rectangle is double the center axis measurement, and the width is double the leg measurement. If a snowflake doesn't have to be a specific size to fit into a project, I don't decide ahead of time how big the completed triangle will be. I let a sense of snowflake aesthetics loose in a fluffy pile of fabric and eventually they crystallize. (To draft the corner triangles, see Example IX, page 63.)

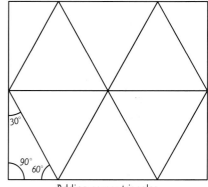

Adding corner triangles

Structurally, a snowflake may be a hexagon, composed of six 60° equilateral triangles, but to uncover its artistic soul, you've got to think of it as a radial design. That's because equal parts of the composition are arranged in a circle. Since the viewer doesn't want to see unrelated chaos, every element in the triangle becomes a directional clue. The eye travels around the circle, making connections between recurrent motifs, searching for the underlying order. The single triangle barely hints at the final hexagonal version and the magic of recurring motifs. In a snowflake design, the whole will be greater than the sum of its parts. It always is.

TEMPLATING

THE CASE FOR GRIDDED TRANSPARENT TEMPLATES

The process you are about to learn is template-driven. By using transparent template material and marking the seam allowance on it, you create a template that functions like a window. This frame allows you to identify the area of the fabric that will be visible in the patch and, particularly relevant to a radial configuration, reveals what part of the fabric bumps into the seamline. The motif that winds up along the wedge's seamline connects to its mirror image. Seamlines will disappear, intricacy will reign, and you will get credit for the magic that happens when the whole becomes greater than the sum of its parts (even when you are just as surprised by the results as everyone else).

The grid overlay on the transparent template material functions as an efficient ruler. To maximize this effect, the lines defining a patch must start and end where two grid lines intersect. A measurement must be clearly identifiable as $1\frac{5}{8}$", not $1\frac{5}{8}$" and a teensy bit more. Points B and C illustrate the difference. Precision plotting ensures accuracy when you have to transfer a measurement from a template to a diagram or make a mark on the right side of the piece-of-the-pie that corresponds to a mark on the left side.

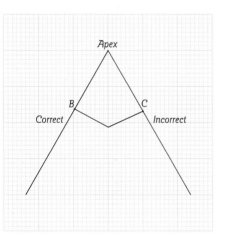

A template grid also helps discipline fabrics that aren't behaving. Some fabrics are bilaterally symmetrical. That is, a line drawn down the middle will divide the design into identical halves. Use the grid to verify that the fabric is evenly distributed to the left and right of the center axis. Pick a doodad, identify its position to the left of the axis, and check to see if its mirror image lands in the corresponding position to the right. It's fabric, not wood. It stretches. Go ahead and give it a little tug to encourage it into alignment.

HOW TO MAKE A TEMPLATE

No matter how complex a shape is, the technique for making a template is always the same. Let's say we want to make a template for patch 2 of our graph paper draft.

Lay a sheet of template material over patch 2, making sure there's enough material to add a $\frac{1}{4}$" seam allowance all around. If the patch straddles the center axis (as patch 2 does here), be sure to align a bold inch line of the template grid on the center axis.

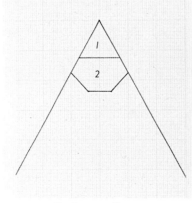

Graph paper diagram

Use a ruler and permanent pen to trace the patch onto the template material. Make sure the lines are dark and legible. They indicate the sewing lines. Anemic lines are ineffectual markers. By the way, did you notice that I slid the plastic down a bit? Since I'm only tracing patch 2 right now, there's no sense wasting the area of the template plastic that covered patch 1.

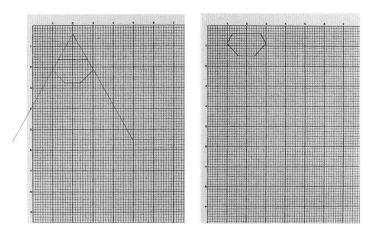

Next, add the seam allowance. On an eight-to-the-inch grid ruler, two lines equal ¼". Align the ruler's ¼" delineation on the edge of the patch so that ¼" extends beyond the patch and the rest of the ruler rests on it.

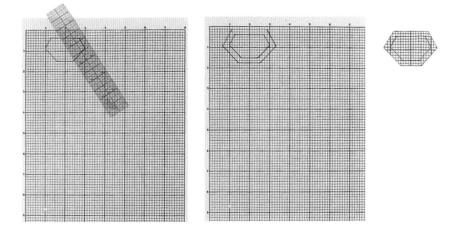

Just zip a line along the ruler edge. Do this all around. Smearing (or schmearing, as we say in the Bronx) is inevitable when a brand-new pen is drawn along the edge of a ruler. It sometimes helps if you wait a beat after marking a line before moving the ruler.

Cut out the template, aiming down the center of the marked line. Once again, the objective is to maintain, not increase or decrease, a template that will be used to cut six identical patches. I use scissors. Use a rotary cutter if it is your cutting gizmo of choice.

Tip:

When adding seam allowance to an extremely acute angle, provide lots of space for the elongated, pointy seam allowance that results.

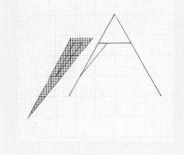

Tip:

On C-Thru rulers (my favorite brand) the measure along the top edge is slightly narrower than ⅛". This variance compensates for the width of a pencil line drawn along it. To determine which edge is up, hold the ruler so the manufacturer's logo is at the bottom. The opposite edge is the top, more narrow edge. Tag this side with permanently marked arrows and use it consistently. If this sounds like the ranting of an overly fastidious technocrat, consider a single triangular wedge composed of ten patches, each with three sides. If an extra pencil line is added with each seam allowance, the wedge plumps up by an additional thirty pencil widths. Multiply this surplus by six wedges and now picture 180 extra pencil widths, joining forces, spreading out, wreaking havoc. Persnickety? I think not.

TWO TYPES OF TEMPLATES

Symmetrical Templates Centered on the Axis

Shapes that are centered on the axis, such as patch 1, are symmetrical and reversible, reading the same from left to right or right to left. When you make a template for a symmetrical, axis-oriented shape, always match the bold lines of the template grid to the corresponding bold lines on the graph paper grid. This simple strategy supports an accurate bilaterally symmetrical, left-right orientation. Marking the shape on the template plastic at random, without regard for the bold lines, cancels out the grid's purpose and may actually confuse you. Once you make a symmetrical axis-centered template, you will use it to cut six identical patches from fabric.

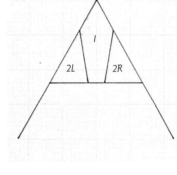

Mirror Image Templates

A shape that sits to one side of the center axis, such as patch 2L, is nonreversible and asymmetrical. These shapes appear in the wedge in mirror image pairs (2L, 2R). That's why the center axis is called the axis of reflection. To obtain the mirror image of such a shape, simply flip the see-through template over. In other words, to cut the twelve fabric patches, you need to make only one template. Use it first to mark six L patches, then flip it over and use it wrong side up to mark six R patches. Sharing the same template is more accurate than making two templates for each pair of mirror image patches.

It is important to mark directional cues on asymmetrical templates so you know which end is up. With many shapes, you'll find the orientation is not immediately obvious once the template is cut out. Without some sort of marking, you risk placing a template higgledy-piggledy on the carefully selected fabric motif or cutting all twelve patches in one direction. Make clue marking part of your template-making routine, as habitual as adding seam allowance.

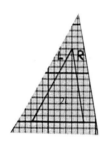

Here's my system. I make templates for the left half of the wedge only. By being consistent, I know every template is correctly aligned to the left side and must be flipped over and used wrong side up to cut the mirror image patch for the right side. To help me orient the template to the diagram, I mark L (for left) and R (for right) at the top of the template. Now, when I pick up the template, I automatically know which end is up. When the L and R are backwards, I know the template is aligned to the right side of the center axis.

Since asymmetrical patches are not positioned along the center axis, it is not necessary to align the bold lines of the grid any particular way. Let the guiding principle for placement—Thou shalt not waste template plastic—be your positioning guide.

HOW TO MARK A TEMPLATE

Once you've decided where to position the template on the fabric, use the permanent marker to trace a few details of the fabric motif onto the template. Choose distinctive eye-catching clues, the kind that will help you identify the position quickly and accurately. Let some of your markings spill across the seamlines into the seam allowance. This facilitates accuracy at the seams, where the actual matching takes place. Make sure mirror image doohickeys land on the grid identically from left to right. Coax them into alignment with a benevolent tug.

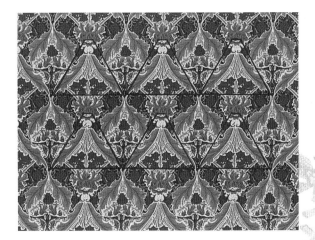

Mark clues on
the template

HOW TO MARK THE FABRIC

Use the clues marked on the template to superimpose the template over the corresponding motifs on the fabric. Trace around the edge of the template with the permanent marker. To mark additional identical patches, align the template on the next available motif and repeat the process.

If you're used to marking the back of the fabric, marking the front may not seem kosher. I do it this way so that I can see the motifs clearly and recognize identical segments readily and precisely. The permanent marker doesn't bleed, and since you cut fabric patches the same way you do templates—by aiming straight down the middle of the marked line—part of the line disappears anyway. Occasionally, my marked lines are indistinguishable from a fabric's printed design lines. If this ever happens to you, turn the fabric over and see if the print is recognizable from the wrong side. If you do end up marking an asymmetrical template on the wrong side of the fabric, be sure to flip the template over too (two wrongs make a right).

In the best possible scenario, the size and shape of your template will allow you to mark one motif and then move the template to the next one without having to skip a partially severed motif in between. But often an irregularly shaped template spills over into the next identical motif, creating the need for twice as many repeats. If you need a more economical arrangement because of how many repeats are available, see if trimming the template produces a more efficient layout without sacrificing the pattern's pizzazz. (If you trim the template, remember to record your changes on the graph paper diagram.) Needless to say, I'm blessed with a holey stash.

Tip:

The thin line of a black permanent marker is practically invisible on the dark blues and indigo of the snowflake palette. Sharpening a light-colored chalk pencil to a fine point in an electric pencil sharpener is an acceptable but imperfect solution, flawed because the point dulls quickly and spreads into an imprecise line. But here's a practical two-step solution: Trace the outline with a white pencil or chalk wheel and then, without removing the template, outline it a second time with the black permanent marker. The thin line of black ink will sit on top of the fat fuzzy chalk mark, distinct and visible.

MY PIECE
POLICY

Designing a snowflake is a collaboration between me, my fabric, and a Bentley photomicrograph. I don't draw random lines on the diagram and then choose the fabric to fill in the blanks. Sewing lines and templates follow my fabric choices, not the other way around. Shape and form may allow the image to be identified as a snowflake, but printed textiles brimming with synchronous color and pattern deserve credit for catapulting the design way beyond the ordinary.

Here's my objective: to create a design that sews together successfully. For me, this means an intricate pattern that fits together easily with no hidden snags while giving the appearance that I know how to sew really well.

Here's my strategy: For as long as it takes to make a snowflake, I'm only going to see and work with one full-size triangle drafted on ⅛" graph paper. This diagram functions as an ongoing, work-in-progress blueprint. It's a detailed plan of action tempered by my palette of fabric. Every sewing line is diagramed. In fact, only sewing lines are allowed on the diagram so that I don't risk interpreting stray lines as seamlines. Since the pattern on one side of the center axis is the mirror image of the pattern on the other side, I don't have to draw sewing lines on both halves of the wedge. Making templates for one side only and flipping them over ensures the lines stay fixed. I mark all my sewing lines on the left side of the diagram. Some people say I do this because I'm a lefty. I think I do it because you read from left to right. You should do what feels comfortable for you.

I know it isn't easy for those not used to drafting patterns to adopt the habit of marking every decision on the diagram. But it's this step that results in a design plan that explains the relationships between all these idiosyncratic patches and ensures they will fit together. Give it a chance. The diagram keeps you honest. Draw every line in pencil so that it can be erased easily, and remember, it's easier to distinguish points if they land on the intersection of two grid lines rather than in between them.

As the design evolves, the patches sew together into irregularly shaped units that combine into bigger sections. The diagram, meanwhile, fractures into a jigsaw puzzle. Three criteria are crucial to success:

❄ *The 60° angle must be maintained along the edges.*
❄ *Every sewing line must be straight.*
❄ *The "i" word must be avoided.*

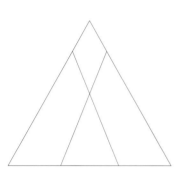

The dreaded "i" word—*inset*— can refer to a Y-seam construction as well as other seamed corners. I never sew into a corner, aptly defined by Webster as "an awkward place from which escape is difficult," because then I'd have to sew out of it, six flawless times. You may sew well enough (I know I don't) to make a few, maybe even several, respectable insets but at least one is bound to malfunction, selfishly pulling the neighboring patches askew along with it. When an inset darkens your piecing horizon—and they will—there is always an alternate solution that pieces together neatly and provides the aspired-for effect (see Example X, page 75). Sometimes you get a bonus, and the problem-solving effort becomes a creative springboard, giving rise to what-if scenarios that you are capable of exploring but never dreamed you were capable of concocting.

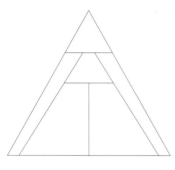

Design a little, piece a little, design a little more. I tend to stay absorbed in the act of designing through two to four fabric choices, at which point my mind's eye overloads. That's when I stop, transfer every decision to the graph paper diagram, make appropriate templates, and cut out at least one patch for each. It's time for a reality check. I can't continue designing without an accurate, up-to-date blueprint. Plus, I need to isolate the chosen motif from the distracting, extraneous, left-out stuff, like wheat from chaff (if my metaphor is wrong, sorry, I'm a city quilter). What is already designed is often the inspiration for the next bout of decision making.

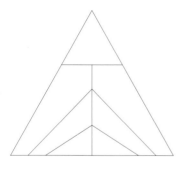

Eventually the diagram may look complex enough to launch something into space, but if you can identify straight lines partitioning the units, the final fit is not unlike a Nine-Patch. Please note, the lines that divide the wedge into sections do not have to follow the graph paper grid.

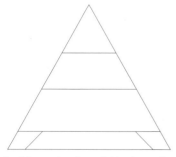

Straight sewing lines divide the wedge into units. Each unit may contain many smaller patches.

I never complete a mock-up of one single wedge before starting the others. Instead, I sew six identical units at the same time, using an assembly line approach. Whatever I do for one wedge, I follow up immediately for all of its mates. By the time the end is in sight, all six triangles are at an identical stage of completion. It's a remarkably efficient piecing arrangement, and not knowing what it's going to look like keeps me engrossed every step of the way.

SEEMINGLY SEAMLESS

My MO is to camouflage seams. Fabricating a snowflake with elaborate details and interlaced patterns means downplaying the fact that it's really a patched together structure built from six separate wedges. Disguising the seams encourages an uninterrupted flow of color and shape from one patch to the next, compelling the viewer to synthesize the components into a visual whole rather than analyze each element separately.

Using fabric this way means freeing yourself from a conventional sense of patchwork. In traditional patchwork, contrasting colors are encouraged at the seams to emphasize the shape of the patch. When patch 1 is indigo and patch 2 is sky blue, the edge between the two is obvious. Such high contrast creates a well-defined line and form.

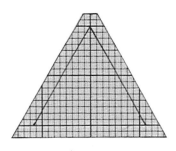 

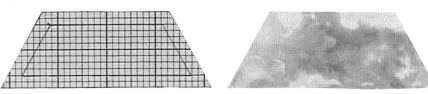

Contrasting colors create a sharp line between patches 1 and 2.

Inventing seamless connections requires a different approach. In the following example, the fabrics for patches 1 and 2 are chosen because their background colors have a bias toward, not against, one another. When the color that functions as the ground in patch 1 connects to a similar color in patch 2, the seamline between them is disguised. Motifs appear to advance and float on a common ground. This illusion is easier to pull off with dark rather than light backgrounds because colors like black, indigo, forest green, and wine tend to blend smoothly into each other.

Similar backgrounds camouflage the seamline.

It's not that I never want to create an area of contrast but that I plan these areas deliberately and judiciously because I am aware of the role they play in the design. When "seamless" techniques are used, the visual whole draws the audience physically closer to the quilt surface, inviting inspection of its organization. The intrigued viewer who gets involved hunting for the seams bears witness to the snowflake's inherent contradiction. What reads from a distance as an integrated whole is discovered to be a highly patched work.

Detail of snowflake on page 12.

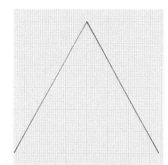

Graph paper diagram

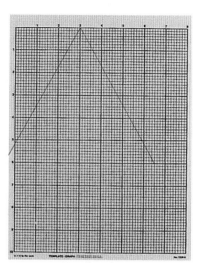

Template plastic
on top of diagram

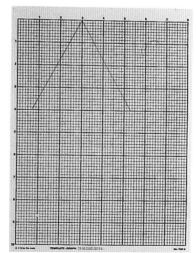

The marked template plastic

WHAT TO DO FIRST

Don't start by deciding how big to make patch 1. Instead, consider patch 1 and patch 2 at the same time. Establishing rapport between the two begins the journey, the process of discovering the design. Picking patch 1 may seem an easier way to get started but, at the end of the day, it's a less efficient way to achieve maximum oomph. Sometimes, I admit, one fabric is plenty. An elaborate fabric filled with nuance and color might be worthy of hefty-sized patches. But usually, six humongous patch 1's multiply into one monotonous hexagon that lacks visual texture.

To explore fabric choices for patches 1 and 2 simultaneously, you'll need to make a window out of see-through template plastic. Start with the 60° angle drafted on graph paper. (I don't want to nag, but be sure the tip or apex falls at the intersection of two bold lines; see page 16.)

Place a sheet of gridded template plastic over the graph paper diagram, making sure to align the bold inch lines of both grids.

Using an extra fine-point permanent marker and ruler, trace 4" to 5" of the 60° triangle onto the see-through template material. Take care to mark as thin and precise a line as possible. Remember, every line has width and length. You don't want to inadvertently increase the width of the template with a pudgy outline.

Keep your finished template intact; don't cut it out, add seam allowance, or draw a horizontal base line limiting the size. Later you can trim it to fit your choices. Reducing a template is easy but enlarging it after the fact means starting from scratch.

THE PATCH 1 PERSPECTIVE

Let's take a minute to contemplate patch 1's unique predicament. It fills up the top of the triangle and eventually takes its place at the center of the design. Since a radial design automatically draws the viewer's attention toward the center, the confluence of six identical patch 1's becomes a focal point *extraordinaire*. This pivotal position assumes a major role, seducing the viewer into the emotional center, setting the climate for the snowflake-to-be. These design duties are fraught with technical accountability.

Patch 1 sprawls from one side of the triangle to the other. At the seams, the motifs meet, match, and reflect themselves into mirror images. Patch 1 bumps into itself not only six times at the center point but also along the left and right legs of each triangular wedge. For this extremely high-profile spot, we've got to pick a fabric capable of delivering, or at the very least promoting, the illusion of graceful seamlessness. To be specific, we need a bilaterally symmetrical pattern, i.e., a motif that can be divided into identical halves by a line passing through the center.

This is *the* spot for a fabric that reeks of compulsive symmetry. I believe that even those of you who don't like symmetry expect a modicum of perfection in the center. In addition to its bilateral properties, a motif worthy of patch 1 must be cut on a straight grain of fabric. Your yardage must be ample enough to yield six of them—so count *before* you mark. The on-grain alignment—center axis of the patch on the lengthwise or crosswise grain of the goods—promotes stability when all six patch 1 triangles are sewn together to form the center of the snowflake. It's the only patch with this requirement. After patch 1, you can throw sewing caution to the wind and indulge your every off-grain fantasy. There will be many future opportunities to consort with asymmetry.

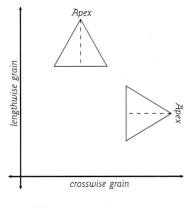

Always cut patch I on-grain

The final shape of patch 1 will depend on the particular motif you choose. The apex must, of course, be a 60° angle, but the remaining edges will be tailored to accommodate the motif. Here are some possibilities:

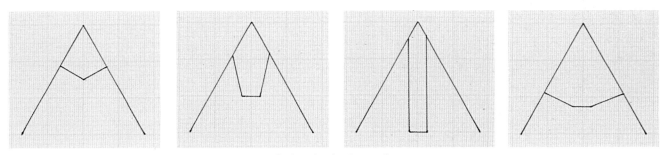

Options for shaping patch I

One more point (no pun intended): See how the seam allowance at the tip extends into a point bigger than ¼"? Imagine the impact when six of these bulked up angles meet in the middle. Don't just snip off the tip willy-nilly. Using a ruler, mark a seam allowance ¼" beyond point A and then cut carefully through the middle of the marked line. (Please note, this is the *only* time you should trim a template's seam allowance without regard for its neighboring template; see Matching Templates for Precision Piecing, page 55.)

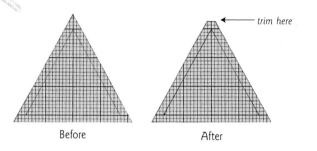

Before   After

LINKING PATCH 1 TO PATCH 2

Let the first and second patches inspire each other. The goal is to find two fabrics that link together smoothly, drawing the eye away from its initial fling with the center and out along new visual pathways. Audition lots of different candidates for patches 1 and 2. Look for connections to obscure the seams for an uninterrupted flow from one patch to the next.

Do I know what I'm looking for when I search my stash? No. What I can tell you is that, instead of looking at a piece of cloth as a whole, I concentrate on the individual elements. Fabrics that look like they landed from different planets often unite in flawless connections, usually because an incidental doodad from one links unexpectedly with a partial motif in the other. It's hard to explain, but you'll know you've crossed over to an altered state of textile consciousness when you find yourself concentrating on the details in a fabric's interior and ignoring the total gestalt.

Paradoxically, this narrowed perspective widens the selection. The secondary components of a print take on an active life of their own. You will probably discover more relationships than you can use. Some connections crackle with drama, while others are so tranquil, it hardly seems worth the effort to sew the pieces together—the result looks like a continuation of the same fabric. But it's not the same fabric, and when multiplied six times, those subtle changes in color and texture will emerge as elegant visual rhythms.

Finding that perfect relationship requires physically manipulating lots of fabrics. To get started, put the fabric intended for patch 1 on your work surface. Next, look for tempting portions of another fabric that suggest a relationship with the first, perhaps because of a similar shape or color. Investigate a possible link by folding the second fabric along the place that caught your eye. Position the fold at the approximate seamline of the first patch. Fine-tune the connection by adjusting the fold. Amend it so fabric 2 sits a little higher on fabric 1. Nope, move it down. More. Hmm. What happens if you turn fabric 2 upside down and coax a relationship from that direction. Nothing? Reach for another fabric and start again. Stop when an appreciative "Ooooh!" slips out of your mouth. This is called the Ooooh Factor. Listen to this involuntary sigh of approval. It usually signals a keeper.

fabric fold

Investigating a link between two fabrics

Have your sheet of template plastic marked with the 60° angle ready to audition the possibilities. Remember, don't cut out the triangle and don't add seam allowance to it. You are now going to tailor templates 1 and 2 to fit the chosen motifs, not the other way around. You'll use the grid of the template as a ruler to measure the size and shape of the patches, making the necessary alterations before doing any cutting.

Place the entire sheet of template plastic on top of the two fabrics, aligning the bold center axis along the center axis of the patch 1 motif.

Ask yourself:

❊ *What lands along the center axis?*
❊ *What lands along the seamlines?*
❊ *What lands in the apex of the triangle?*

An auspicious, enticing beginning will connect to itself six times without causing the word *murky* to come to mind. Move the template plastic around to check out different possibilities. What happens if the template starts a little higher? Now what lands on the axis and along the seamlines? Once you've decided on the final version, trace hints of the motifs from both fabrics to the template using the permanent marker. Do this immediately before things shift, or you'll headtrip that you've lost this "perfect" spot forever.

The marked template plastic

Now look through the template plastic and locate the seamline between patches 1 and 2. Remember, it is easier to rely on a measurement if the line travels from grid point to grid point. Adjust the template as needed and then mark the line on the template. "But," you protest, "if you've already marked the clues, it's too late." "It's never too late," I answer. "But repositioning may mean new templates."

Using the template as a ruler, count down from the top of the triangle to measure the distance from the apex to the patch 1/patch 2 seamline. Here it's 2¼". Transfer this measurement to the graph paper diagram by counting down 2¼" from that triangle's apex. Draw in the seamline on the graph paper diagram.

Now you can focus on shaping patch 2. Its bottom contour doesn't have to be a horizontal line from one side of the triangle to the other. Often the central motif connects smoothly with patch 1 but the stuff on the sides is boring or filled with smiling yellow sun motifs that just don't say "ice crystal." If you don't want 'em, whack 'em off.

I use short 6" rulers to shape patch 2. The idea is to frame the area you want to be visible in the patch. Position the rulers on top of the template and move them around, using the straight edges to isolate portions of the motif and define potential shapes for the template. Remember to lay the rulers so the outlines they form start and end at points of intersection on the grid. Once you reach a decision, don't remove the rulers. Hold them firmly in place and draw lines along the straight edges to form template 2. Transfer these lines to the graph paper diagram by counting off the grid lines.

Using rulers to shape patch 2

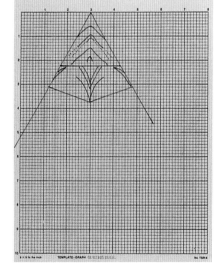

Master template

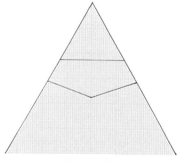

Graph paper diagram

Let's peek ahead and compare some completed patch 2's. In the patch 2 just drafted, the distance from the apex to the bottom edge (excluding seam allowances) is 3¾" (3⁶⁄₈" on our ⅛" grid) along the center axis and 3⅛" along each side seam. The resulting bottom edge ends in a wide point.

In this next and slightly smaller variation, the distance from the apex to the bottom edge is 3⅜" along the center axis. Instead of coming to a point, the edge travels 1⅛" to the left and right, then veers up and connects to the same 3⅛" point on each side seam. If I'm not sure how I want to shape patch 2 and I don't mind wasting fabric, I'll make a template fit the bigger option and reevaluate it later.

Once you've designed and drawn in patch 2, your master template can be turned into either template 1 or template 2 but not both, because there's no way to accommodate two sets of seam allowances at their mutual connection.

If you decide to turn it into template 1, your next step is to make a real live template 2 with seam allowance, before cutting the master apart. How? Put another piece of template material on the master template and trace template 2 using a ruler and a permanent marking pen. Add the seam allowance and cut out the template. Align the new template 2 precisely on top of the original template 2, and trace hints from the original.

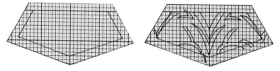

Now go back to your master template and add seam allowance to template 1.

Cut out template 1 from the master template.

Here's a sneak peek at the finished center. In real life, you would not sew the six units together at this point. Some more examples of patch 1/patch 2 connections follow.

LINKING PATCH 1 TO PATCH 2
Center A

B. The Diagram

Fabric 2

1

2

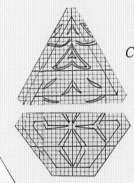

C. Templates 1 and 2. The edges that will join are trimmed at the corners for accurate alignment (see page 55).

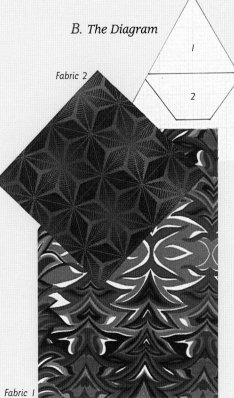

Fabric 1

A. The Palette. Fabric 2 is a directional pattern rendered as a three-dimensional design. Including the gradual shading adds complexity when the wedge is multiplied into a radial structure.

D. Patches 1 and 2, with seam allowance. The white inverted V toward the bottom of patch 1's center axis pops like a curvy mustache, creating the illusion that the two patches aren't interrupted by a seam. The bright accents will become important directional clues, causing the eye to travel around the circle and search out recurrent motifs.

E. Patch 1 sewn to patch 2, with seam allowance.

F. The result, sewn together prematurely for your viewing pleasure.

LINKING PATCH 1 TO PATCH 2
Center B

B. *The Diagram*

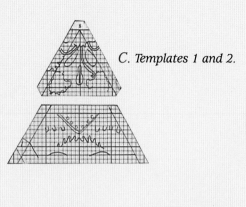

C. *Templates 1 and 2.*

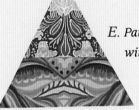

D. *Patches 1 and 2, with seam allowance.*

E. *Patch 1 sewn to patch 2, with seam allowance.*

A. *The Palette*. My choice was to winnow out the kelly green motifs in fabric 1 or use this unsnowflakelike color sparingly.

F. *The result*. The connection between the patches doesn't seem seamless... until the complete hexagon is revealed. Fabric 2 packs the patch with dots, dashes, and shadings that add up to a bundle of energy.

LINKING PATCH 1 TO PATCH 2
Center C

B. The Diagram

A. The Palette.

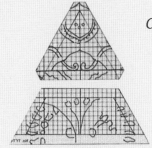

C. Templates 1 and 2. Note that some of the markings spill across the seamlines into the seam allowance. This facilitates accuracy at the seams, where the actual matching takes place.

D. Patches 1 and 2, with seam allowance. Here's an example of using two extremely similar fabrics. When viewed together, the patches seem like a continuation of the same fabric.

E. Patch 1 sewn to patch 2, with seam allowance. Joining the patches maneuvers the design into elegant rhythms neither fabric was capable of on its own. The motifs seem more curvaceous than angular, but once these sparkling shapes and shades entwine, they set the stage for the extensions at the wedge's corners.

F. The result.

LINKING PATCH 1 TO PATCH 2
Center D

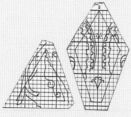

B. The Diagram

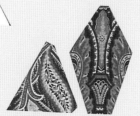

C. Templates 1 and 2.

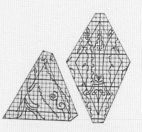

G. Templates 1 and 2 revised.

A. The Palette.

D. Patches 1 and 2, with seam allowance.

H. Patches 1 and 2 revised.

E. Patch 1 sewn to patches 2L and 2R, with seam allowance. My original idea was for patch 1 to end ⅛" to the left and right of the center axis, rather than in a sharp point, for a less bulky seam allowance. But the ensuing shape included too much black motif at the connecting seam, resulting in a less continuous link between the patches than anticipated.

I. The revised patches sewn together.

J. The result.

F. The Diagram revised. I reshaped the bottom of template 1 to remove the black motif. Now template 2 ends in a point on the center axis.

SHAPING TEMPLATES TO FABRIC

Now you're ready to start thinking about patch 3. Take a look at patch 3L in the example below. This position is perfect for an intricate motif that can be flipped into a mirror image. It requires twelve mirror image repeats, or six clones that wiggle to the left and another six wiggling in reverse. Since it isn't patch 1, the laws of fabric grain are moot. The question is, how do you get the motif you want to wiggle right into your patch?

When I look at intricately patterned fabric, I see the design aligned the way it was styled, typically in a top-bottom, left-right orientation. What I'd like to be able to do is contort myself like a rubbery super hero and explore it from every possible perspective without leaving my seat. (My alias could be Rubber Maid.) My mind's eye isolates fragments of patterns, trying to predict which one would metamorphose into something spectacular when joined to its mirror image along the triangle's side seam.

Well, I'm no super hero, but put a see-through template in my hand and I'll sound as clairvoyant as a fortune teller with a crystal ball. Without a template, I'm powerless.

Since at this point I don't know how big patch 3L will be, I make the template bigger than it probably will end up and trim it to fit the chosen motif directly on the fabric. Start by identifying the template's position in relation to surrounding patches. In this case, side x attaches to patch 2 and side y settles along the side seam and will eventually connect to its mirror image. Whatever lands along the remaining two sides will affect our fabric choices for future patches.

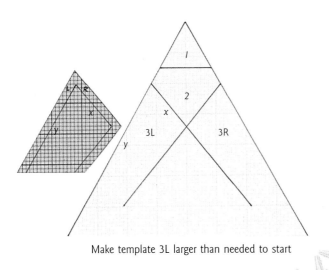

Make template 3L larger than needed to start

Audition links between patch 2 and a potential fabric 3 by physically placing the fabric against patch 2's seamline.

Audition potential links

If you don't know where to start, look at the fabric as a whole. Start where your eye is caught, perhaps by a warm glow or dramatic blush of singular color. Let the template take you into nooks and crannies that didn't seem interesting before. Move it a teensy bit to the right to catch a shadowy beam, tweak it to the left to include a curl. Then pick it up and try again.

Use the template to view different possibilities

A patch that bumps into its mirror image along the seam inherits certain idio-syncrasies. For one thing, the amount of pattern automatically doubles. Keep this in mind. Too much of even a good thing can end up boring. On the other hand, a single spark or glimpse of color punctuating the triangular wedge sets off a visually exciting chain reaction as it encircles the finished block. Here's a sneak peek at three variations (don't actually sew patch 3L now or a dreaded inset will be set in motion):

Using the same bilaterally symmetrical fabric three different ways

With this type of template making you could plop an entire motif in a patch—but would you want to? Do you really want the audience to identify butterflies fluttering in the middle of your snowflake, or do you want them to experience the gestalt? Sometimes, a larger image multiplied six times equals boring while multiplying a fragment yields a unique, imaginative bit of intricacy that never existed before. Because it is unexpected, the effect seems more spontaneous, less contrived.

Promise me you won't take it personally if this search for the perfect motif takes a long time. Become the little search engine that can. Your mind's eye learns an awful lot during this quest, even if it's receiving angst-ridden messages that the process is taking way too long and it's all your fault. Sometimes, to get from a boring "here" to an inspired "there," you have to make a lot of stops in between.

POWER STITCHING

HOW TO STRIP-PIECE VERY SMALL PATCHES

My personal lexicon divides printed fabrics into two categories: directionals and allovers. A one-directional design has a distinct top and bottom, which means that patches cut from it must be carefully oriented in the same direction. I affectionately refer to these high-maintenance textiles as "prima donnas." Simultaneously temperamental and charismatic, these fussy cuts are the divas that give the design its distinctive voice.

Allover, nondirectional designs, in contrast, look exactly the same from any angle. An allover's forgiving temperament makes it the fabric of choice for piecing lilliputian patches accurately and efficiently. Here's where we unravel the mystique of sewing itsy-bitsy patches.

The rule is simple: Never make a template for one lonesome allover. A patch comprising a single allover fabric does not need its own template. Allovers are cooperators, willing to share templates with their neighbors for the common cause. The trick is to strip-piece, except it is not a trick; it is an uncommon practice based on common sense. Long story short: Sew a strip of the allover fabric to its neighbor (it could be a patch, a pieced unit, or another allover), make one template incorporating both patches, and mark and cut out both simultaneously.

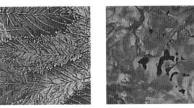

Allover nondirectional fabrics

Example I

I want the intricate motif selected for patch 3 to float on the background. To create this effect, I based my fabric choice for patch 4 on the background color of prima donna fabric used for patch 3. (See Seemingly Seamless, page 27.)

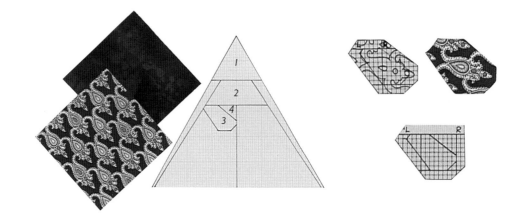

1 Make a template that encompasses patch 3 and patch 4. Add a ¼" seam allowance all around, and cut out. Using a ruler, extend the seamline into the seam allowance at each end to ensure accurate placement along the full length of the sewing line. Align template 3 + 4 on template 3 and transfer the hints.

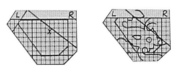

2 Rotary-cut one or two strips of fabric 4. The strip(s) must be large enough to accommodate six 4L and six 4R patches, or 12 patches altogether. (See How to Calculate the Width of a Strip, page 49.)

3 Place side *x* of patch 3 on the fabric 4 strip, right sides together, and machine-stitch. Repeat, sewing all the units at the same time, assembly line style. Remember that six units must be reversed.

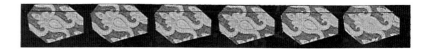

Piecing Key

+ Sew the fabrics together
• Patch sewn and cut from two fabrics

4 Press the seam allowance toward the wider patch. Position template 3 + 4 on one stripped-together unit. Match the hints drawn on the template to the corresponding motifs in patch 3. Align the sewing line marked on the template with the seam made in step 3. Hold the template firmly in place and trace around it to mark a visible, precise line on the fabric 4 strip. Cut out patch 3 + 4, aiming the scissors down the middle of the marked line.

5 Repeat step 4 until you have twelve accurately pieced units, each one complete with seam allowance and ready for its next assignment. In honor of the occasion, I give it a new name: patch 3·4. Doesn't it look as if tiny patches were meticulously cut and pieced together?

Power Pressing

I press after every piecing sequence. My objective is twofold: (1) to press seams toward the bigger patch and (2) to press them into submission.

Example II

Here's a slightly different scenario. In this case, both patch 3 and patch 4 will be filled with allovers. Because there is no prima donna fabric involved, neither patch needs its own template.

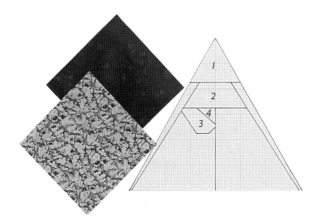

1 Make template 3 + 4, add a ¼" seam allowance, and cut out. Extend the seamline into the seam allowance.

2 Rotary-cut strips of both fabrics.

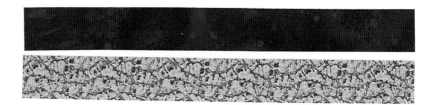

3 Sew the two strips together. Press the seam allowance toward the larger patch's fabric.

Piecing Key

\+ Sew the fabrics together
• Patch sewn and cut from two fabrics

4

Position template 3 + 4 on top, aligning the sewing line marked on the template with the seam made in step 3. Trace around the edge of the template. Repeat to mark six 3 + 4 L patches. Flip the template over to mark six 3 + 4 R patches. Cut out.

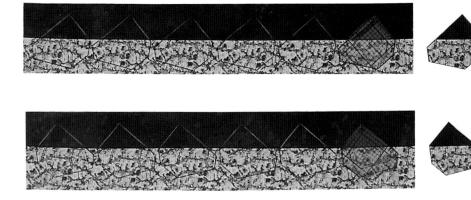

How to Calculate the Width of a Strip

Place a transparent ruler on the template so that the ruler's ¼" demarcation (two ⅛" boxes in from the ruler's edge) rests on the seamline. In other words, ¼" of the ruler falls on one side of the sewing line (representing the seam allowance) and the rest of the ruler lies on the portion of the template that represents the piece to be added on. Read the ruler measurement at the widest part of the template. In this example, patches 3 and 4 both require 1¼"-wide strips.

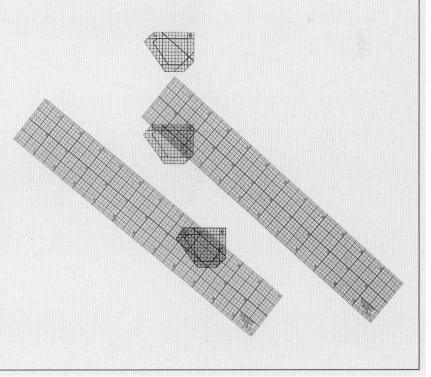

Example III

This time I want to add an allover to the left and right sides of patch 2. Patches 1 and 2 are both prima donnas.

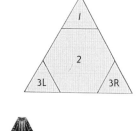

1 Make template 3L + 2 + 3R, add a ¼" seam allowance, and cut out.

Trace a few fabric hints from patch 2 to the template.

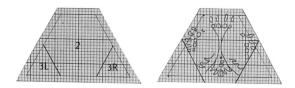

2 Rotary-cut one or two strips of fabric 3, enough for 12 patches.

3 Working assembly line style, strip-piece the lower left edge of each patch 2 to the fabric 3 strip.

4 Press the seam allowance toward the wider patch. Position template 3L + 2 + 3R on one stripped together unit, matching the hints and the lower left seamline. Trace around the patch 3L portion of the template and cut on the marked line. Repeat to make six pieces total.

5 Repeat steps 3 and 4 to strip-piece patch 3R to the lower right edge of each patch 2.

Here's a sneak peek at the final version. If you stopped here, you'd have an 8" hexagonal plate snowflake made up of three fabrics. Usually I continue adding many more pieces.

Example IV

This example is for Master Level Power Strippers. The plan is to fill each of the eight numbered patches with an allover fabric. Speckled patches represent the background fabric. When you need to strip-piece an enclave of allovers, you'll use half as many templates if you start from the center and add on in both directions.

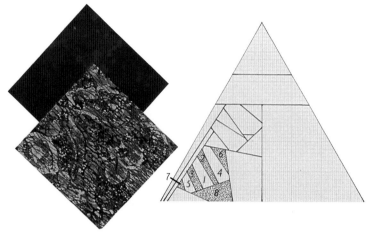

1 Make the following four templates:

Template 1 + 2
Template 3 + (1 + 2) + 4
Template 5 + (3 + 1 + 2 + 4) + 6
Template 7 + (5 + 3 + 1 + 2 + 4 + 6) + 8

Each template will be used to strip on two patches, first to one side and then to the other. As you proceed, the pieced unit will grow in size.

2 Sew patch 1 + 2:

Cut long strips of fabrics 1 and 2 and machine-stitch them together. Position template 1 + 2 on the strip-pieced unit, aligning the marked line on the seam. Trace around the edge of the template. Repeat to mark six L units total. Flip the template over and mark six R units. Press. Cut out. You should have twelve 1·2 patches.

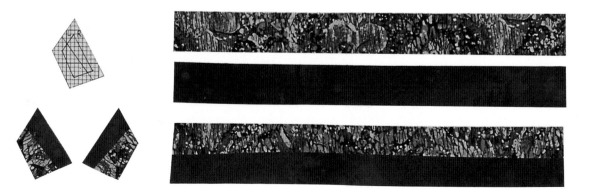

Piecing Key

+   Sew the fabrics together
·   Patch sewn and cut from two fabrics
·· Patch sewn and cut from multiple fabrics

3

Sew patch 3 + (1·2) + 4:

Strip-piece fabric 3 to the fabric 1 edge of each 1·2 patch. Press. Align template 3 + (1 + 2) + 4 on top. Trace around the patch 3 portion of the template and cut on the marked line. Repeat to mark and cut six L units, then flip to mark and cut six R units. Add patch 4 to the fabric 2 edge in the same way. You should have twelve 3·1·2·4 patches.

4

Sew patch 5 + (3·1·2·4) + 6:

Strip-piece fabric 5 to the fabric 3 edge of each 3·1·2·4 patch. Press. Align template 5 + (3 + 1 + 2 + 4) + 6 on top. Trace around the patch 5 portion of the template and cut on the marked line. Repeat to mark and cut six L units, then flip to mark and cut six R units. Add patch 6 to the fabric 4 edge in the same way. You should have twelve 5·3·1·2·4·6 patches.

5

Sew patch 7 + (5·3·1·2·4·6) + 8:

Strip-piece fabric 7 to the fabric 5 edge of each 5·3·1·2·4·6 patch. Press. Align template 7 + (5 + 3 + 1 + 2 + 4 + 6) + 8 on top. Trace around the tiny patch 7 portion of the template; repeat to mark and cut all six L units, then flip to make the six R units. Strip-piece fabric 8 to the lower edge of patch 7·5·3·1·2·4·6 (it joins to five patches). Press toward patch 8. Align template 7 + (5 + 3 + 1 + 2 + 4 + 6) + 8 on top. Trace around patch 8 and cut; repeat to make six L units and six R units. You should have twelve 7·5·3·1·2·4·6·8 patches. As you've no doubt noticed, the string of numbers denoting multiple fabrics can grow quite long. Shorthand turns "patch 7·5·3·1·2·4·6·8" into "patch 7··8."

THE FINE POINTS & PERKS OF STRIP PIECING

Master Piecing

The very best reason for strip piecing is obvious: You look like a piecing wizard. You can add diminutive, uncommonly shaped pieces to your design without having to cut and stitch impossibly tiny patches. Remember, never make a separate template for a patch designated for strip piecing.

Trueing Up

And here's the second best reason: the opportunity to trim patches to the newest template. I try my best, but between sewing and pressing and handling, stuff stretches. Every new template made to guide a strip-piecing procedure is an opportunity to retrim the piece-in-progress, correct its irregularities, and pull it back in line with the graph paper diagram. Assume the newest, just-made template is accurate. Align the template to the patchwork and trim off any fabric sticking out beyond the template. I trim a lot, often using the handy-dandy Brooklyn Revolver, a circular rotary mat mounted on a lazy Susan.

Alignment

Always align the template to the prima donna. It's the fussy fabrics' job to convey the snowflake's repetitive internal formations. Follow the hints marked on the template to ensure that all six patches are the same. Next, position the template's sewing line directly on top of the actual seamline. If you have to fudge—and you will—make amends with laid-back allover prints. Don't worry if an allover is a little bigger on one side than the other. When this happens, let it. The irregularity will energize and animate the image.

Grain Matters

Use strip piecing as a stabilizer to lend tangible support to a patchwork assembled from mostly off-grain pieces. A stabilizing quality is added to the whole shebang every time a strip cut along the grain is used.

Trimming Seams

Check out the wrong side of this patch. See how the seam allowance extends beyond the necessary ¼"? Use common sense and trim off the excess tidbits. Strip-pieced units usually need to be pruned.

Pressing Issues

Sewing narrow pieces means the ¼" seam allowance is sometimes bigger than some portion of its patch. Put a passel of puny patches side by side and the excess bulk starts bumping into the sewing machine's seam guide, causing it to bounce off its straight path. To prepare multiple layers for smoother stitching, press after every piecing sequence, toward the bigger patch if possible, making each seam lie as flat as possible. Sometimes you're forced to press toward the smaller patch. For instance, if a bunch of seams already coexist in a tight area, it may be impossible to press the just-sewn strip in any direction except the way it naturally flops. In these cases, go with the flow, and press as flat as you can using all your body weight.

MATCHING TEMPLATES FOR PRECISION PIECING

Sometimes you have to piece one irregularly shaped patch to another. The problem is that the techniques learned in traditional patchwork—match the edges and corners and then stitch—don't work when shapes with different angles are joined together. When you join a square to a square or a half-square triangle to another half-square triangle, the angles patched together are the same. But with irregularly shaped patches, odd and differently angled shapes abut each other and need to be stitched along a common seam. We don't care what the angles are. We just want them to fit together as effortlessly as a Nine-Patch.

Wild Goose Chase is a traditional design with this precise predicament. Sewing the two triangles together should be a piece of cake, but somehow you end up with mud pie. Align the patches right sides together, side *x* to side *y*.

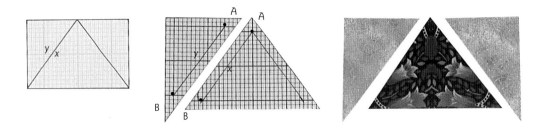

Uh-oh, here's the problem. The angles at the two point A's are different. Ditto for the two point B's. When you align the cut edges of two differently angled shapes, the resulting patch is distorted. There is no guideline that helps you position the fabric shapes together accurately. The sharper the angles to be pieced, the more difficult it is to eyeball the correct alignment. Here are two attempts that failed. In the first, I tried to align the bottom edges of both templates. In the second, I aimed for the top.

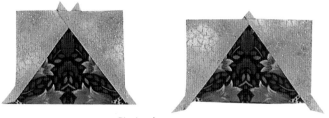

Piecing by eye

Actually, estimating is never a viable option. We need foolproof. Once again, the solution is provided by see-through templates with seam allowance and sewing lines marked.

Example V

Patches 2 and 3 are to be pieced together.

1 Make templates 2 and 3 as usual. I cut the fabric patches to show you what the shapes look like, but do not cut yours just yet.

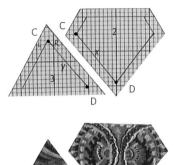

2 Place template 2 and template 3 right sides together, as you would two fabric patches. Align the sewing lines *x* and *y* and match points C and D at each end. Once the two templates are precisely aligned, look closely at the template plastic in the vicinity of point C. See how a little triangle of extra plastic on template 3 sticks out beyond template 2? I have no idea why, but I call these tidbits of template, that peek past a significant other, dog-ears.

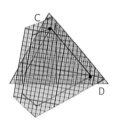

Using the rigid edge of template 2 as a guide, mark and trim off the excess dog-ear.

3 We're not finished yet. It's not enough to know where to start. The other end of the sewing line must also correspond. An accurate match extends from cut edge to cut edge. Otherwise, you don't know what to aim for and can end up stretching a patch too much or not enough. So, repeat steps 2 and 3, this time addressing the area around point D. The templates are now ready to cut fabric patches that will piece together perfectly.

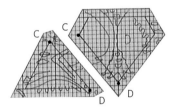

Example VI

Sometimes the difference between the two corners is a minuscule sliver of plastic. Trimming this dinky excess will not produce an edge-to-edge match you can really count on. Such a small amount can easily be overlooked or misunderstood, seen more as a faulty scissor snip than a deliberate alteration. In situations where there isn't an obvious dog-ear, you should make one.

1 _____

Invent a new blunt angle on either template, preserving approximately ¼" seam allowance. Mark and cut.

2 _____

Align the templates right sides together and sewing lines matching. Trace along the newly cut edge to mark the identical angle onto the second template. Trim. When this operation is complete, two previously dissimilar corners are now the same.

Consider these grooming techniques a cardinal procedure. Neat and tidy templates with evenly matched edges are crucial for accurate piecing alignment. Never assume the corner angles of neighboring templates are identical, and never assume they match "enough." Templates either match each other, or they don't. Align every template to its adjoining template, right sides together, sewing line to sewing line, and trim away any plastic peeping past its partner. You'll shed excess seam allowance, waste less fabric, and, by arranging patches cut edge to cut edge, eliminate the need for pinning before stitching. What have we learned from this? Templates made from see-through material are good.

ADVANCED TEMPLATE MATCHING

The above discussion assumes you have access to both neighboring templates. But sometimes, you need to cut patches from a template before the adjoining shape is designed. If there's an overabundance of seam allowance stored in its corner, common sense urges you to trim the surplus before you waste all that yummy fabric.

STOP! If you trim it without coordinating it to its neighbor, you risk shortchanging the amount of seam allowance needed. The result might be an impossible-to-compensate-for-gap in the final seam, even if you deliberately leave a generous amount. Chances are you will clip it at a sensible angle, parallel to the template grid, while the required slant is more wacky and impossible to predict.

Example VII

Patches 2 and 3 will be sewn together along the AB seam. No matter what the future holds for the space labelled 3, you can trim template 2 now. You'll need the graph paper diagram, the template, a ruler, and a permanent marker.

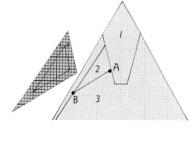

1 To get oriented, position the template on its corresponding shape on the graph paper diagram. Flip it over, right sides together and the AB seamlines matching, as if you were going to sew patch 2 to patch 3.

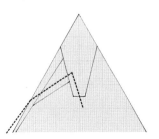

2 On the graph paper diagram, locate the current boundary of patch 3. Now, if this seamline had a ¼" seam allowance added to it—the way templates do—you would be able to use the edge of the seam allowance to trim the point of the template. So, with a ruler, add the seam allowance line in very light pencil, knowing that you want to erase it ASAP. It's shown here as a blue dashed line.

3 Realign the template facedown on the diagram, as in step 1. See the little triangle of plastic near point B that extends beyond the penciled seam allowance? Using the penciled line as a guide, mark and trim off this protruding tip. Immediately erase the simulated seam allowance. Remember, only actual sewing lines are allowed on the diagram. You can now rely on the template's cropped edge to cut out patches primed for proficient piecing.

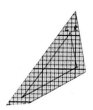

AVOIDANCE BEHAVIORS

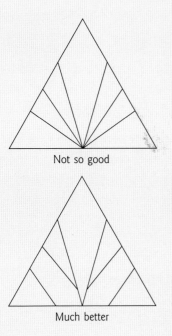

Not so good

Much better

No

Yes

Avoid Bulky Construction Sites

Circumvent a multitude of seams wherever possible. When I see three or more sewing lines about to crash into the same destination, I reroute the drafted lines to avoid a collision. Of course, there are times when this kind of detour isn't possible or desirable. There are also times when rethinking the design because of these considerations makes it even better.

You are the boss. You put the pencil lines there. You can take some away. Strike a balance between the patterns the textiles suggest and the network of pencil lines. If the final version doesn't fit together, or if it is just plain sloppy, it won't matter how drop-dead gorgeous the original vision was.

Avoid Obsessing Over Points

Patchwork etiquette favors well-matched points and equal-sized patches. Our quiltmaking legacy is filled with sharply defined points. But unconventional shapes are more in line with a snowflake-inspired design, simulating the spontaneous development (and disappearance) of an ice crystal buffeted about in a blustery atmosphere. If you're the type that needs permission not to obsess over points, a close look at a photomicrograph will give you a valid reason to rethink point protocol. Photomicrographs reveal that snowflakes aren't full of sharp points at all. The shapes are tapered but they aren't sharp and crisp. Instead they seem blunt, rounded, and imprecise.

Matching and stitching thin shapes with acute angles is difficult enough without worrying whether two lines must always meet at the same spot. Try reshaping severe points into more user-friendly forms by redrafting pointy tips so they meet ⅛" or ¼" apart. Or, simply accept that it is okay for these kinds of points to join together unevenly—and some inevitably will. Irregular stabs of color make the design more natural, more transient, more in motion.

Evaluate every narrow point drawn on the diagram. Sometimes a fabric's lovely details end up eliminated when an elaborate motif is crammed into a tight area. Use intricate fabrics to their best advantage by applying a windowlike template and following the route of the print. Sharp points destined to rendezvous along the side seams are rendered best in simple allover prints. Then the assembly process does not demand matching both an intricate pattern and seam joints.

Avoid Insets

An inset is a corner of frustration filled with potential doom. Set-in corners are not set in stone. Use the diagram to map an alternate stitching route.

FINISHING TOUCHES

JOINING TOGETHER

Theory

This is the moment we've been waiting for. The whole becomes greater than the sum of its parts, and we finally get to witness the magic we have wrought. Keep in mind that success in the snowflake genre is not about matching every single joint along all twelve borders. A few mismatched points are simply not going to be noticed in a patchwork filled to the brim with complexity. The objective is to identify which junctions will be the most disruptive if they are slightly off. Season the usual rules of piecing with a generous dose of common sense. Remember, visual coherence is already guaranteed by the symmetry of six identical sections radiating from a central point.

My policy is to spoil the prima donnas and fudge with the allovers. In the snowflake scheme of things, the fussy cuts usually cluster toward the attention-grabbing, mood-setting center of the hexagon, so I concentrate my efforts there. Examine the finished triangle along the seamline and locate areas of maximum value contrast. For example, a white line sitting against an indigo background makes for a strong contrast. Since the eye zooms in on areas of sharp contrasts, align these junctions carefully. The coupling between areas of soft contrast can be mildly awry, even downright crooked, without dissolving the illusion of seamless continuity from one wedge to the next.

Practice

Place two wedges right sides together, matching the corresponding patches and seamlines, and pin. Use thin, sharp silk pins. Basting doesn't seem to make the alignment more accurate, especially when there are big bulky seams along the presser foot's intended route.

Begin by matching patch 1 at the apex of the triangle to its twin in the second triangle. Next align the prima donnas and areas of strong value contrast. Finally ease in the more forgiving allovers. Gently, but with forceful assurance, aim for neatly joined seams.

Sew slowly, using small stitches. Begin from the skinny tops of patch 1 and sew toward the bottom, backstitching at the beginning and end. If the presser foot bumps off the ¼" seam, stop. Rip. Remove any leftover threads. Realign. Repin. Restitch, overlapping a few of the leftover previous stitches with new ones.

Example VIII

Here's the piecing sequence for a six-sided design:

1
Sew one triangle to another. Press the long seams open.

2
Stitch a third triangle to this pair.

Stop and examine your work. This three-triangle unit forms half of the hexagon. If a hexagon comprising six wedges equals 360°, then three wedges joined together equal 180°. The base of a 180° arc is a straight line. Therefore, three triangles stitched together must form a straight line. If your triangles look like this:

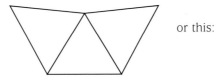 or this: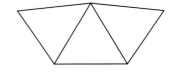

then don't expect them to join together in 360° harmony. Analyze and correct the blooper before going on to steps 3 and 4. The error is probably due to an inaccurate seam between two wedges. A Master Template without seam allowance (see page 62) might be useful.

3
Repeat steps 1 and 2 to make the second half of the hexagon.

4
Align the two halves right sides together. Pin at the seam joints and where important motifs meet. Pay particular attention to the juncture of all six patch 1's in the middle, and the patch 1/patch 2 seam joints. Stitch the two halves together, starting and ending with a backstitch. Press the long seam open.

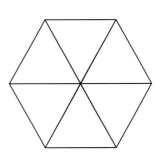

REPAIR STRATEGIES
Master Template with Seam Allowance

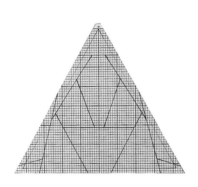

You can rehabilitate a flawed piece-of-pie with a Master Template. Line up a sheet of template plastic to the graph paper diagram, matching the center axis of the diagram to a bold inch line on the template plastic grid. Trace the 60° angle onto the template plastic. Copy a few of the longest or most vital sewing lines. Trace enough lines from the original to provide clues for aligning the Master Template to the piece of patchwork pie. Add seam allowance. A big wedge may require two sheets of template plastic taped together (make sure you align the grids). Or, make a template of one half of the triangle and flip it over to investigate the other side.

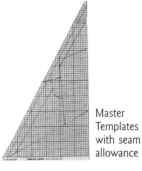

Master Templates with seam allowance

To use a Master Template, place it on the pieced wedge and align the all-important on-grain patch 1 and the center axis. Don't expect every clue to match a sewing line. Now, assess how and where the pieced triangle is off. Sometimes the seam allowance along the side seam is too narrow or too big. Sometimes, identifying one unruly seam as the culprit is enough to adjust the design. Sometimes the mature, sensible thing to do is take a deep breath, rip, and repair.

A triangle that ends up too big can't be automatically fixed by chopping off the excess at the side seams. If the guilty party is an allover fabric, whack away, fitting the shape to the Master Template. A little more/a little less won't make much of a difference. But never trim a fussy cut that's primed to meet its identical twin without weighing the consequences. If only one is trimmed, the joint between two mirror image motifs is no longer the same. It's okay if one of twelve connections doesn't match. But if a pack of prima donnas is threatening to ruin the production, try a Master Template without seam allowance.

Without Seam Allowance

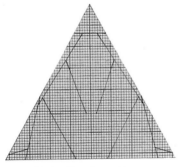

Master Template without seam allowance

Another remedy for healing a warped wedge is to mark the side seam sewing lines on the wrong side of the finished triangle. Otherwise, there is an assumption that the edge of the completed fabric triangle is accurate and can be used to align to the neighboring triangle. For this remedy, you'll need to make a full-size Master Template without seam allowance.

Align the Master Template to the wrong side of the fabric triangle, first to patch 1, then to the center axis, then along a couple of the long seams. Hold the template firmly in place and trace around the edge with a well-sharpened lead or chalk pencil or a somewhat dried-out permanent marker. The idea is to make a visible but pale line that doesn't bleed through to the front.

Next, align the marked triangle with its partner, right sides together, pinning together where the marked sewing line coincides at a seam joint. Sometimes marking both triangles is helpful even if only one is inaccurate. If the resulting seam allowance is very narrow—less than 1/4"—use a small stitch length and go over it a few times to reinforce the join.

CORNER TRIANGLES

As we discussed earlier, adding a right triangle to four of the six wedges turns a hexagon into a rectangle (not a square), ready to frame or combine into a quilt. Calculating the dimensions of this 30°-60°-90° corner triangle requires no gadgetry. It simply equals one half of the piece-of-pie.

Example IX

1 Draft a 60° triangle on graph paper the same size as your wedge diagram. Draft a horizontal line left from the apex along the grid line.

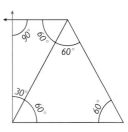

2 Now draft a vertical line up from the lower left corner of the wedge. The two lines will intersect at a 90° angle.

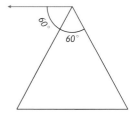

3 Note that the vertical leg of this new corner triangle is the same length as the center axis. Make a plastic template of the new triangle, adding ¼" seam allowance to each edge. You will need to cut four corner triangles—two L's and two R's (reverse the template)—to complete your hexagon block.

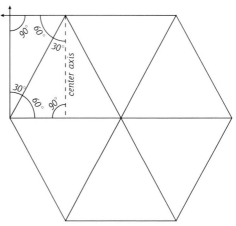

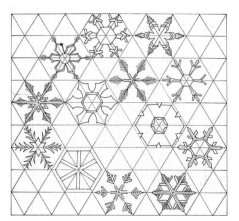

A triangular grid

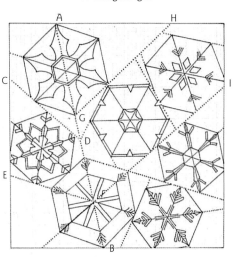

A random composition

Hexagon layout in a hooked rug

LAYOUT

There's a perk to working with hexagons. Six-sided blocks can be arranged in a traditional pyramid quilt. Work out the composition on a triangular grid, putting background fabric in the empty triangles. If your snowflakes are different sizes, base the grid on the biggest wedge. Let's say the largest snowflake is built from 10" wedges and the smallest has 8½" wedges. Add 1½" of background fabric (plus seam allowance) to each 8½" wedge to up the size to 10".

A more random composition is also possible, with long seams dissecting the quilt into major parts. See how seam AB cuts the quilt in two? The left side of seam AB is subdivided by seams CD and EF. Seams GH and FI divide the right half of the quilt into three sections, which are further subdivided by straight lines.

I've kept this magazine clipping of a hooked rug on my bulletin board since 1993. It offers an accommodating layout for hexagonal blocks.

QUILTING

I quilt by hand with a hoop in my lap, marking the quilt pattern as I go. Chalk lines show up better than penciled ones on a surface crowded with multicolored patches. Since I don't want my imperfect stitches to show, I choose a thread color that blends with both the front and backing fabrics.

I try to devise an accommodating pattern that unites the various areas of the quilt yet has built-in flexibility. Long quilting lines fracture the background of *Kaleidoscopic XI: Snowfall* (page 6). Where two long lines intersect, I added two short ones about four inches long, creating a six-pronged starburst at the junctions. Three differently sized hexagons—the base triangles measure 1¼", 1½", and 1¾"—pepper the ground of *Kaleidoscopic XXII: Ice Crystals* (pages 8–9). Some stand alone; others are partially imposed on one another. In both quilts, one or two quilting lines echo a shape or line in the actual snowflakes.

This kind of flexibility lets me adapt my stitching path as needed, depending on whether I am in the thick of the seam action, or leisurely meandering along in the more open background spaces. Generally, I quilt more in the background and do very little stitching in the actual snowflake. You don't want to get bogged down in a field of seams.

I like the soothing rhythm of hand quilting. But the real reason I don't machine-quilt is because I don't know how. My esteem for those who do it well is on par with my admiration for great writers of fiction. I wish I could wake up on my birthday and know how to machine-quilt without the hurdle of a learning curve. (I used to wish I would wake up on my sixteenth birthday with straight hair like Joan Baez. Check out my author photo. I guess I'd better set aside some quality time to learn how to machine-quilt.)

PART 2
THE ARTFUL SNOWFLAKE

INTERIOR DESIGN

Choosing a theme from nature means working with immediately recognizable subject matter. But my goal has never been to hold a mirror up to nature and reproduce the realism of a photomicrograph. I don't make snowflake quilts because I love snowflakes. I make snowflake quilts because I love to make quilts. The content conforms to the process. I use the techniques and materials of quiltmaking to communicate the lacy, three-dimensional beauty of an ice crystal, shaping the theme to fit my medium, not the other way around.

Thanks to commercialism, most of us think of the snowflake as a visual paragon, a model of perfection. But how can a drifting ice crystal be perfect? It gets blown around in an active environment. Flitting through clouds, colliding with its fellow crystals, it gets acted upon by shifting winds and temperatures.

Erasing nature's irregularities suits a craft sensibility that strives for perfection. But it is imperfection—not perfection—that renders a more animated, less mundane effect. Snowflakes are interesting because of, not in spite of, their flaws. For a patchwork snowflake that steps beyond pure technical prowess, you've got to leave in some quirks and irregularities. The final image must target the viewer's sense of a snowflake: cold, delicate, unique. Make use of this instinctive human response. Play to these common denominators.

THE ANATOMY OF A SNOWFLAKE

Extensive study of the fold-and-cut white paper snowflakes plastered on early childhood classroom windows reveals two important snowflake facts: There is a similarity in general shape while there is also an endless variety in structural details. From an early age, we know one thing to be true: No two snowflakes are alike.

Snow crystals' distinct markings are made not by colors (since a crystal is colorless throughout) but by formations that alter the path of light passing through them, thus causing relative areas of light and dark. Ridges, grooves, cavities, and water films are identifiable markers caused by specific conditions. Ridges are thicker than other portions of the crystal and function like miniature convex lenses. Grooves seem to occur where branches partially weld together. Cavities, responsible for the greatest number of lines and dots, are usually empty but sometimes partially fill with water. Water films produced by slight melting cause wavy scallops.

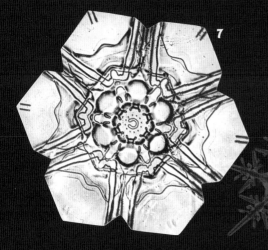

SNOW CRYSTALS

I. Hexagons

Simple hexagonal plate, 1
Large hexagon with simple extensions
at the corners, 2, 4, 6, 7, 9

II. Stellar Crystals

with formations at the ends, 5
with broad branches, 11
with dendritic extensions, 8, 10
with fernlike extensions, 3

Christmas tree

Grandma's brooch

Chicken feet

Think of it. A slight fluctuation in temperature causes snow to fall to earth in countless original mini masterpieces. When a hexagonal crystal grows at –15°C, new ice causes the corners to stick out a little bit and sprout arms. These extensions occur because ice forms more rapidly at the corners of the hexagon than along the flat sides. Since the six corners are all the same, the six protrusions resemble one another too. A slightly lower temperature here, more humidity there, and new features come into view, in the same exact place, on each of the six arms.

As the ice crystal contends with different atmospheric conditions, it matures into a unique and intricate individual. The foliage decorating the extensions becomes so idiosyncratic and marvelous, it's easy to envision a team of angelic master sculptors, giddy and giggling as they one-up each other. Some formations resemble miniature Christmas trees, others look like chicken feet, and the variety detailed like faceted jewels are reminiscent of brooches last seen on grandma's bosom. To convey all this delicate complexity in fabric, we've got to identify the essential characteristics and common elements. Reproducing every detail is not necessary, but hinting at the abundance of detail is. Isn't that what much of the wonder is about—a natural phenomenon adorned with intricacy, emerging from a symmetrical core?

There are numerous official lists compiled by atmospheric scientists that sort the hundreds of forms into groupings. The most complete, by the late Dr. Choji Magono of Hokkaido University, Sapporo, Japan, lists 78 types of snow crystals. For design purposes, I've devised my own simplified classification based on general appearance. There are two major categories: hexagons, also called hexagonal plates, and stellar crystals, which can have large or small hexagons at the center (see pages 68–69).

HOW TO BUILD A SNOWFLAKE

Now we get to use all this information to make patchwork look like snowflakes. Take off your spectator's hat and assume the designer's perspective.

Start by choosing background fabric. Its unassertive role may be the most important because by connecting into continuous negative space, it organizes and defines the shape of the snowflake. Ground cloth lands along the center axis and peeks in and out of the branching shapes. The more complex the extensions, the more background is needed. The more background that is used, the more fragile and lacy the effect. (The more lacy the effect, the tinier the patchwork and the more tedious the piecing.) See Common Ground (page 90) and Figure & Ground (page 94) for more specifics.

Inventing the six-sided nucleus, or center, comes next. Patch 1 and any other motifs that visually attach to it become the hub. Sometimes it ends up a large, generous hexagon and sometimes it's barely discernible. I come to this moment with no preconceived notion, giving my fabric stash carte blanche to ignite something serendipitous between a few fabrics. (See Linking Patch 1 to Patch 2, page 32.)

The center unit is usually the first to be designed and the last to be pieced in the wedge. When this is the case, the sextuplets that make up the center get set aside until the end, when the other sections that form the wedge are fitted together and the top unit has something to piece onto. It's not unusual for the design sequence to differ from the piecing sequence. It depends on how the wedge is organized into segments by straight sewing lines.

After creating a center from prima donnas ready and able to take on the task, and recording the seamlines on my graph paper master diagram, I slow down long enough to pick a snowflake model. An actual image of a snow crystal is an invaluable tool. Let it guide you toward shapes and contours that are most characteristic of snowflakes, so that you can, in turn, lead your audience to irrefutable snowflake recognition. It doesn't matter if the center of the crystal is similar or completely different from the one already designed. I often create a composite based on more than one image, then modify the cumulative sketch depending on what fabric is available. To sharpen your study, isolate one of the six triangles from the hexagon. Analyze the general contours that form its distinctive silhouette. You're not going to replicate it so just grab enough basic information to guide you.

Next, draw a line down the center axis of your graph paper triangle and interpret this line as a seam. Read that last sentence again. (This is one of those moments where, if I were standing in front of a class, I'd make sure I had eye contact and everybody heard me.) From this moment on, the design focus shifts away from the center axis to the triangle's sides. That's where the glamorous extensions occur, the stuff that inspires poetry and deserves hyperbole.

Isolating one wedge

Extensions

Survey the various configurations that function as extensions in the snowflake images throughout this book. Most extensions seem to have a core that stands out, as if containing a narrow inner tube that glows brighter than its surroundings. The eye, caught by the luminous extremities, jumps from one piercing jab to the next. Sometimes thin, sometimes broad as if multilayered, extensions seem embossed with darkened grooves and ridges. Some remain the same width from top to bottom, others taper into delicate points or dissipate, giving way to more elaborate formations. Simple extensions translate easily in a single fabric, while complex ones need a mix of prints to render the play of light and dark.

Choosing fabric for the extension is the next important decision. Within a mostly monochromatic color scheme, a light color doesn't have to be very saturated to become an accent. I designate one of the lightest colors in the palette to illuminate this position, always an allover and always user-friendly cotton. Even if I'm aiming for a shimmery, glimmery effect, I don't use a textile that needs to be interfaced. Extensions are exceedingly narrow patches accompanied by an entourage of seam allowances that are about the same width, creating an underside dense with extra fabric layers. Press the inevitable thickness as flat as possible and ignore the unavoidable imperfections.

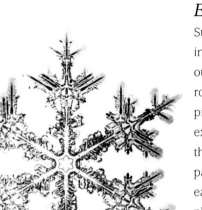

These extensions seem to glow brightly at the core

Use luminous allovers for extensions

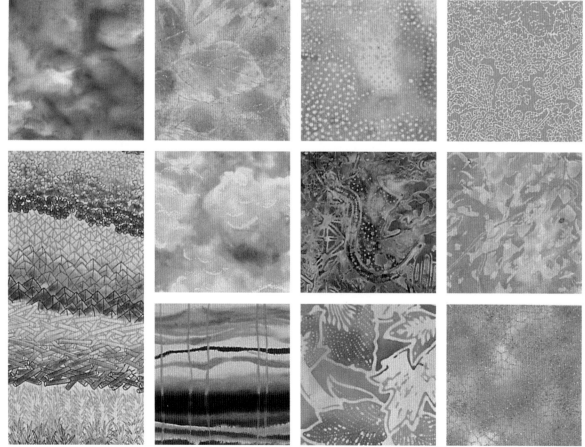

Extensions form at the center hexagon's corners and grow out. Draft them down the legs of the triangle, starting below the patch or patches that designate the center of the hexagon. Since extensions land along the side seams, they bump into themselves, multiplying into twins. That's why an allover is the fabric of choice—the assembly process doesn't demand matching both an intricate pattern and seam joints. Patches landing along the central axis will either visually connect to the center unit or attach to the extension, depending on the choice of color. A similar color conveys continuity while sharp contrast calls attention to a new theme.

Once again, the design and piecing sequences differ. Stripping the extension to the left and right sides of each wedge is a last step. This step may look awkward, especially with a long slim extension, but consider the benefits. Stripping an allover fabric to the side seam is a chance to even out previous glitches. It functions like a barricade, keeping fabrics inside the extensions from crashing into themselves. Nothing has to match. In addition, since they don't touch each other, fabrics don't have to be perfect mirror images. They can be symmetrical wannabes and still perform like attention-getting, eye-catching divas.

Here's how to strip the extension to the patched-together unit. Make a template big enough to include both extensions, stretching from one side of the triangle to the other (yes, you have to add seam allowance). Or, if you want, draft the extension on one side of the template only and flip it over for the mirror image. There's an advantage to this one-sided template. The side without the extension is the exact size of the wedge's interior patchwork. Use it to true up both sides before stripping on the extensions.

extension

To create elaborate extensions, sketch lines on the graph paper diagram modeled after a specific snowflake, then use a ruler to revise sketchy outlines into distinct straight ones. Strike a balance between an engaging image and one that seems pieceable. The more the wedge is broken up into patches of snowflake and patches of background, the more complex the extensions become.

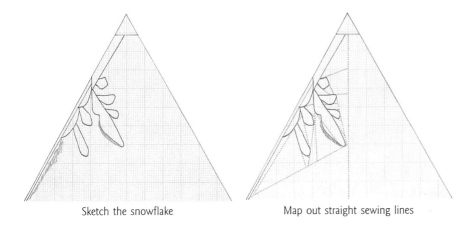

Sketch the snowflake   Map out straight sewing lines

Sometimes one clever hunk of fabric fills the niche instead of a mix of fabrics, often a fabric printed on a ground cloth similar to the snowflake's background color.

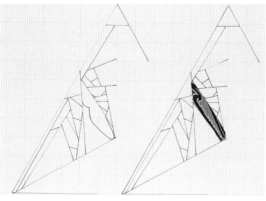

Mostly Hexagons

Large hexagonal plates (see pages 68–69) are a lot like traditional spiderweb or kaleidoscope blocks. The six 60° triangles fill up almost completely with the snowflake fabric. This design may not knock your socks off but it is in fact the kind that occurs most frequently in nature, when temperatures are low and the growth of crystals slow. Supposedly, these were Bentley's favorites because he delighted in the internal ornamentation.

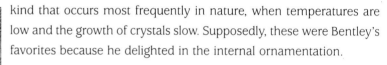

It's easy to decode a large hexagon with simple protrusions once a single triangle is isolated from the six-pack. A little background fabric injected along the center axis toward the last inch or two of the triangle is all it takes. Decide on the size of a single wedge, let's say 4". Design from the apex down, stopping 1" to 1½" from the base of the triangle. Draft a line on the center axis from this point down to the base. Design the patches for the simple protrusion and designate the remaining areas to be filled in with background fabric via strip piecing, as shown in the sample wedges here.

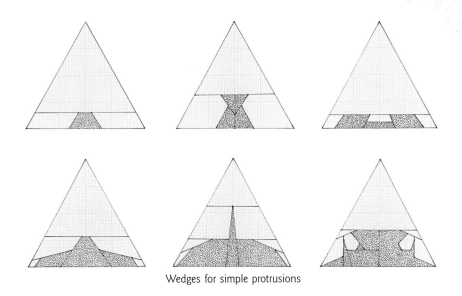

Wedges for simple protrusions

Example X

Three prima donna patches—I'll call them A, B, and C—will combine into a single protrusion. The remaining area will be background fabric, which means A, B, and C can be strip-pieced. I use short rulers to straighten and extend the sketched-in lines, trying to figure out the most direct sewing map with the fewest seams.

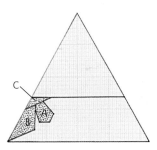

1 I rejected my first attempt because I inadvertently created an inset.

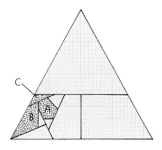

2

My second attempt corrected the inset, but I didn't like the minuscule sliver between patches A and B.

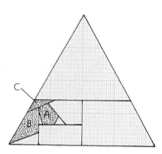

> **Piecing Key**
> + Sew the fabrics together
> • Patch sewn and cut from two fabrics

3

I worked out a piecing diagram that avoids an inset. This version would require six templates:

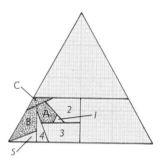

(A + 1)
(A + 1 + 2)
(A + 1 + 2 + 3)
(4 + A + 1 + 2 + 3)
(B + 5)
C + (4 + A + 1 + 2 + 3 + B + 5)

Here's the piecing sequence:

Strip 1 to A
Strip 2 to (A·1)
Strip 3 to (A·1·2)
Strip 4 to (A·1·2·3)
Strip 5 to B
Sew (B·5) to (A·1·2·3·4)
Strip C to (A·1·2·3·4·B·5)

4

I continued revising the diagram, this time omitting the center axis seam. This version also requires six templates:

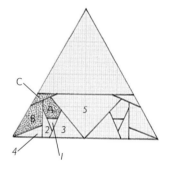

(A + 1)
(A + 1 + 2)
(A + 1 + 2 + 3)
(B + 4)
5
(A + 1 + 2 + 3 + 4 + 5 + C)

Here's the piecing sequence:

Strip 1 to A
Strip 2 to (A·1)
Strip 3 to (A·1·2)
Strip 4 to B
Sew (B·4) to (A·1·3·2)
Sew 5 to (A·1·2·3·B·4)
Strip C to (A·1·2·3·B·4·5)

5

Here, patch A has seven sides instead of six, for a softer, rounder effect. The bad news is that patches 1 and 2 are microscopic. If I want to keep this shape, I would rework the stitching lines once more, attempting to enlarge patches 1 and 2 while making as few seamlines as possible. Or I might look for a fabric that conveys the rounded shape without seams, as on page 74.

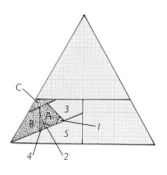

Mostly Extensions

Photomicrographs reveal a rare snowflake form with an itty-bitty center and long exposed limbs. These stellar shapes may not be the most characteristic of snowflakes but there's something elegant about this less-is-more form.

A snowflake with six intricate, branched extensions projecting from a small hexagon is the universal prototype. A well-formed dendritic snow crystal has six main arms that are 60° apart, with branches angling 60° from each arm, and sometimes smaller branches on these branches. The most prominent branches often occur at the same distance from the center of the crystal on each main arm. The minor branches usually start more randomly. In other words, perfectly symmetrical drawings are not entirely realistic.

Rendering the sumptuous effect of branching or plumelike extensions is a combination of effective fabric choices and lots and lots of strip piecing. It's easier to describe what the shapes aren't than what they are. Shapes are rarely pointy; they are slightly rounded. Branches aren't perfectly parallel to each other as if synchronized; instead, the spaces in between are always a bit uneven. I'm warning you. An inkling of randomness is harder to convey than uniformity but well worth the effort. Reveal the snowflake's irregularities and you unleash its realistic spirit.

THE COLOR OF SNOWFLAKES

When it comes to color in fabric, I am a strong proponent of a "more is more" approach. Add to this the fact that I am not a purist and you'll understand why it pains me to admit that a snowflake palette must be disciplined by color restraint.

While a snowflake is colorless and transparent, the ideal of snow is immaculate whiteness. My path toward self-appointed quilted ice crystal maven began with the notion that a six-sided, blue and white quilted kaleidoscope would look like a snowflake. I wasn't smitten with an urge to convey gossamer translucence or study crystallography. I wanted a vehicle for gorgeous, charismatic, patterned textiles. My color sensibility told me that in order for a bunch of fabrics to arrange themselves into the semblance of a snowflake, they had to be blue.

I now declare with conviction what was once just intuition: Patchwork snowflakes are of a bluish persuasion. The audience assumes that blues are cool colors and recognizes a chilly crystal thriving in a wintry mood. If you love red and you love snowflakes, this is not an occasion when you can have it all at the same time—not if you want it to read like a snowflake. Instead it will register as a six-sided reddish kaleidoscope, which is not necessarily a bad thing, but not the goal here. Figure out what you are aiming for, understand the color ramifications, and make an informed decision. I feel obligated to say that when it comes to red, purple, or green snowflakes, students in my classes have been there, done that, and regretted it.

Having sung the blues, let me now make clear I am not advocating a strict, compulsively unyielding, monochromatic color scheme. Chill out. Don't get too rigid. Stick to this color family, but with flexibility. Aim for diverse blues, silver and white against a dark indigo ground, with grayed violets and bluish greens as accents. If it catches your eye, try it. There is no such thing as the blue and white police.

Remember, you're matching seams, not colors. Perfectly matched colors can be boring. Comparable colors create sophisticated visual connections by establishing a relationship between the parts. Even if each and every shape is colored without regard to the others, the final version will be seen as shapes and areas that overlap and interweave.

A print that is primarily shades of icy blue might be peppered with twinkles of green or purple. These don't make the fabric unusable. Use a see-through template to isolate the snowflake shades and either edit out the delinquent ones or apply them sparingly. Sometimes a small surprise enhances the palette, pushing it from everyday to delicious. Accents function like spices. Seasoning the design with an unexpected glimpse of color enhances the flavor. Realize I'm talking about colors used as elements on a background, not as the background. If the background is kelly green, nix it.

Icy colors tinged with green, pink, or brown

Kaleidoscopic XI: Snowfall (page 6) is filled with much more color than initially meets the eye. When I asked a couple of textile stylists to catalog the colors in the quilt, they found blues named sapphire, indigo, royal, cobalt, ultramarine, denim, periwinkle, iris, aqua, navy, baby, sky, sea, cerulean, Windsor, delft, Prussian, turquoise, and peacock. Use these last two sparingly. (They also spotted blue-gray, pale gray, steel gray, slate, shale, pewter, tin, chromium, aluminum, mirror, smoke, mauve, mustard, lavender, violet, and rose.)

The first time I demonstrated Snowflake A (page 103), I intended to apologize for the flash of turquoise that tagged along with the main motif in template 1. I had agonized over whether or not to squelch this impulse, knowing in its central position it would multiply into six times more than a twinkle. There I was, in Fairbanks, Alaska, facing quilters on intimate terms with snow. Before I could open my mouth, one of the quilters asked: "How did you know? How did you know that glaciers are turquoise?"

Fabric for patch 1 of Snowflake A

When serendipity plops undeserved credit in your lap, seems like a good time to keep your mouth shut.

Now let's discuss white. When students express concern that an in-progress design seems dark, I know the next thing they're going to want to do is throw light on the subject. Literally. They immediately assume a white or light-colored fabric is the antidote. A light-colored fabric is not necessarily going to create lightness or brightness. It is going to create a startlingly distinct shape if the fabrics next to it are on dark grounds (see Seemingly Seamless, page 27).

I'm not saying never create distinct shapes and I'm not saying never use patterns printed on a light-colored background. I'm only saying, in this design instance, there are more efficient design pick-me-ups. For example, light colors sprinkled on dark backgrounds sparkle, producing an effective stimulant. Think of stars twinkling in a night sky. Enough said?

A QUILTER'S GUIDE TO SNOWFLAKE FABRIC

MATERIAL WHIRL

Picture the two of us hanging out in your sewing room. I'm the curly-haired one wearing black (what did you expect? I'm from New York City). I'm also the one pulling fabric from your stash and pushing you to try lots of them where you thought one would be plenty. Just so you know, here's my agenda: to balance my sense of what a snowflake looks like with my heartfelt belief that when it comes to fabric, more is MORE!

In an 1889 issue of *Appleton's Popular Scientific Monthly*, W. A. Bentley wrote "Great as is the charm of the outline, the internal ornamentation is far more wonderful and varied. All of the specimens exhibit in their interior most fascinating arrangements of loops, lines, dots and other figures in endless variety. So varied are these figures that, although it is not difficult to find two or more crystals which are nearly if not quite the same in outline, it is almost impossible to find two which correspond exactly in their interior figures."

If that doesn't sanction using as many different prints as is humanly possible, I don't know what will. Nature combines skill and artistry to fashion these transient crystals, each with its own unique beauty. While I want to keep to the fundamental spirit of the parameters identified and documented by Bentley, my concern remains the appearance of a snowflake translated in fabric. I know I can't reproduce every detail of the natural shape in patchwork, no matter how tiny I make my pieces. That's why I rely on intricately printed fabrics to render an image filled with complexity.

This is when we establish guidelines—not rules—for translating this pure gem of nature into fabric. My approach to fabrics is selective and excludes preconceived notions of what goes with what. Making a match between incongruent fabrics makes my day. Go ahead. Commit random acts of fabric!

The dictionary definition of "to match" is to be exactly alike. But using only stuff that is the exact same creates a flat, insipid effect, not the lively, complex nuances that transpire when light and shadow play nicely together. Variety in a single block provides visual texture. My inclination is to balance glamour and usefulness. When possible, practice *piece*ful coexistence by placing a forgiving textile next to a fussy one. Consider the weight and fiber content of adjacent fibers. Good fabrics make good neighbors.

Don't think that when I sit down at the kitchen table I know what's going to happen. (That's where I work in my family's two-bedroom New York City apartment. Instead of a studio art quilter, does this make me a kitchen art quilter?) Sometimes I'm in brainstorm mode. I flit, I fly, my mind's eye wanders through the big mud pile of fabrics that spills from the table onto the floor. Whatever catches my eyes ends up in my hand. I can skim and discard ten fabrics in a New York minute. Other times, I'm obsessive-compulsive. Something in the collection calls out that it deserves serious consideration, and I sit there and work it to death, making it unravel its hidden potential, just for me.

SHOPPING KARMA

I swear this is true. I heard on National Public Radio that they figured out where the material instinct is located in the brain. (My husband suggests they may have actually said "maternal instinct.") Well, if there is such a thing, it proves human beings have a natural predisposition to acquire material, and, obviously, some of us have better developed gray matter than others. I love printed textiles. Stick me in a shop brimming with bolts and my fingers instinctively reach out to fondle the goods, igniting a lovefest.

If you're going to develop a knack for material pursuits, you've got to have an attitude. Never make excuses for the size of your stash. Be your own advocate. Cloth is as valid a palette as any other medium.

I am not a purist. I look for medium-weight, firmly woven fabrics, exploring the treasures of New York City's garment district the way people in Maine check out Marden's, Bostonians remember the first Filene's Basement, and Bronxites brag about the original Loehmann's on Fordham Road under the Jerome Avenue El. Practice a "grab-it-when-you-see-it" strategy. Quilt lore is filled with legends about the fabric that got away. When something grabs your eye, grab it back. Don't stop to question a material instinct. When asked, "What are you going to do with that?" just smile knowingly. Personally, I feel sorry for the ones who don't get it.

In the past couple of years, I've developed a vocabulary that labels patterned textiles according to personality and function. There are two basic categories: prima donnas and allovers.

THE PRIMA DONNAS

Prima donnas are powerful design elements. Also known as fussy cuts, they are temperamental, charismatic, and often, though not necessarily, symmetrical. Any motif that needs to be duplicated exactly and needs its own template is classified a prima donna. Basically, a prima donna is a fabric that can't be sewn on via strip piecing. It's a high maintenance fabric that, accordingly, needs to be lavished with attention. In exchange, its unique voice makes a memorable statement.

To determine how much yardage to buy, I begin by counting off six or twelve repeats. The reason for the double amount is that patches not centered on the center axis need two mirror image motifs per wedge. Keep in mind that odd-shaped, off-grain patches can spread across two repeats, requiring double the doubled amount, especially when the repeats are close together. I usually end up buying one yard of a small repeat and two of a big one. When you find a highly stylized arabesquelike fabric generously covered with interlaced motifs set far apart, you'll feel like you're buying acreage in order to guarantee enough repeats, but the potential for mesmerizing designs makes it worth the investment.

Here are some different types of prima donnas that I have identified:

On-Grain Motifs with Bilateral Symmetry

I covet patterned textiles printed with perfect bilateral symmetry. A bilaterally symmetrical motif can be divided into identical halves by a line passing through the center. When the pattern on one side of the line is flipped over along this line and superimposed on the other side, the match is identical. The motion is called reflection, and the line is called an axis of reflection.

These intricate, ordered, formal patterns are the treasures of my fabric stash. The interplay caused by the repeat is magical. Examples include classic Liberty of London designs, synonymous with the Art Nouveau movement, foulards, and prints from my Benartex fabric lines. The term *foulard* originally referred to a lightweight silk cloth block-printed in small-scale patterns. But now the name refers more to a pattern of small, evenly shaped geometrics.

On-grain motifs in set layout with bilateral symmetry

My collaboration with Benartex, Inc., stirs together everything I love about colorful patterned cloth into fabrics that tickle my imagination and earn their keep: intricately entwined designs, abundantly colored in vivid hues and set in mirror image repeats; elegant, charismatic patterns tinged with the promise of countless quilts to come; versatile fabrics that work well with an eclectic mix of printed and dyed textiles; fabrics that sometimes set the stage and sometimes dance on it. Thanks to the skills of the Benartex staff, I often get what I want.

Bilaterally symmetrical patterns are ideal for patch 1. The agile motifs soften the straight lines of the long seams, creating the illusion of graceful continuity. Magic takes place when elements along each of the wedge's sides connect to their mirror images and blossom into something brand-new.

Symmetry fabrics by Paula
Nadelstern for Benartex

1. #633 "Shimmer"   2. #631 "Palazzo"   3. #635 "Marble"   4. #636 "Bali"

Pseudosymmetricals

Some fabrics turn out to be symmetrical wannabes. I call them pseudosymmetricals. This means they give the appearance of symmetry at first glance, but a closer inspection reveals differences between the two sides.

Pseudosymmetricals can be gorgeous and useful so don't banish them from your stash. For every good fabric there is a time and place. But since it's not a pretty sight when bad things happen to good fabrics, identify the sticky wickets where these symmetrical pretenders inevitably self-destruct. Don't position a motif lacking true bilateral symmetry where it is expected to match itself perfectly along both left and right seams simultaneously. If the two sides of the motif are different, they can't connect seamlessly to their mirror image no matter how hard you try, chant, or pray. *Never* push one of these into a patch 1 role.

Where can you use pseudosymmetricals? Look for occasions where a patch isn't destined to meet itself coming and going. Place it along the center axis but don't let the patch extend all the way from one side of the wedge to the other. As long as a direct confrontation with its mirror image does not occur, a somewhat-symmetrical fabric will imitate symmetry and the discrepancies will not be noticed. The eye interprets the rhythmic repetition of elements as symmetry even if the motifs are a little lopsided.

Sometimes the junction between two quasisymmetrical patches can be manipulated to neutralize the disparity. This solution depends on getting one set of the motif's edges to meet in an accurate mirror image either at the seamline or along the center axis. The rest of the patch will flow away from this joint in a slightly different way to the right than the left. No one will ever notice as long as the connecting seam between the two is clean and continuous. Treat the faux-symmetrical motif as if it's the real thing by using only one template even though the hints on the template don't quite line up when it's reversed and flipped over.

Another option is to inject an interruption. If you don't want a patch to touch its mirror image, pierce the flow of pattern with something else, preferably an allover that can be stripped on. Patches destined to rendezvous along the side seams are rendered best in simple allover prints anyway. Then the assembly process doesn't demand matching both an intricate pattern and seam joints.

Pseudosymmetrical patterns

Zingers

Eye-catching, irregular motifs often interject vivacious punctuation points that read as identical when the eye travels around the snowflake. Use lively asymmetrical motifs as accents in patches that aren't destined to meet themselves. The viewer is drawn again and again to look for the hidden surprises.

Zingers

Mirror Image Motifs

A fabric printed with pairs of mirror image motifs is a rare and useful find. Often, figures that appear to be oriented identically to the left and right turn out to be the same motif rendered right-side-up and upside-down. This is often true of paisleys, with its characteristic teardrop shape. Its typical allover layout in which the forms flow around each other in elaborate profusion disguises the fact that it's really the same paisley facing in the same direction over and over again. Check it out by tracing hints from the fabric on template plastic. Flip the plastic over to see if you can find some motifs facing the opposite way. Do this before you cut out six in one direction. Otherwise you'll end up with the equivalent of two left sleeves.

A paisley that truly wiggles to the left and the right offers a strong sense of movement. Any of its off-grain motifs reflect into exciting effects brimming with animated details. Sometimes I am so enticed by the potential, I create a patch too generous in size and cross the line from enticing to overwhelming or even worse, boring. Then I go back, whack some off, and strip in something else.

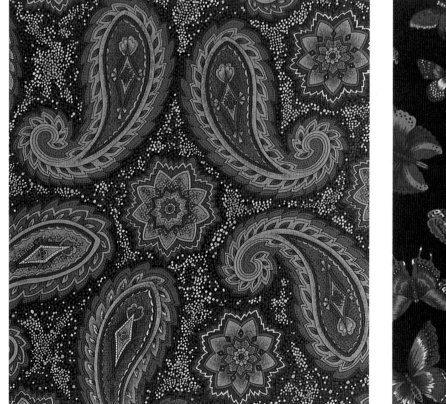

Mirror image paisleys   Butterflies with mirror image wings

Directionals

Directionals include stripes, zigzags, and wave patterns. One-directional designs have a distinct top and bottom—all the patches must be cut facing the same direction—but two-directional prints could be turned upside-down and no one would notice. Directionals can be arranged neatly in rows, in grids, or on the diagonal. Zigzags and serpentine stripes infuse a more lively quality than herringbones and chevrons, but their erratic behavior makes them difficult to use bilaterally and in small shapes. Plus wavelike and serpentine aren't exactly terms that come to mind when describing a snow crystal. Audition the curves but don't be seduced into letting them take over the design. Straight lines are usually what you need to foster the sense of a snowflake.

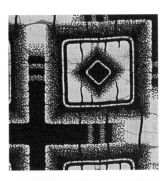

I thank my fairy god shopper when I find a directional pattern rendered as a three-dimensional design. Ombré is the textile designer's term for patterns distinguished by gradual shadings and blending of one color into another. These great organizers make adept transitions, adding complexity while carrying the viewer's eye smoothly from one form to the next. Attaching a shadow to a basic stripe sets off vibrations that defy the fabric's flat surface.

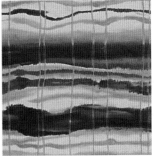

Ombré shading

Stripes are useful two-directional prints because they automatically slide the eye from here to there, forming visual pathways that instill an element of motion. Sometimes stripes become fussy cuts and sometimes they are surprisingly good candidates for strip piecing. Also surprising is the fact that the outcome doesn't seem awkward or misaligned when a stripe collides haphazardly into itself at the seam.

Stripes

I particularly like to strip on skinny straight bands of color. Realize there are two ways to strip a stripe. The effects are completely different if cut parallel or perpendicular to the selvage, so audition which way you prefer the stripe positioned in the patch. Sometimes I lightly sketch in the options on the graph paper diagram.

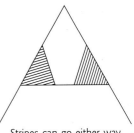

Stripes can go either way

ALLOVERS

An allover is the prima donna's friend and facilitator. This nondirectional design looks exactly the same from any angle. It has no implicit top or bottom, left or right, and there are no demanding mirror image or bilaterally symmetrical motifs. The allover's forgiving temperament makes it the pattern of choice to take on a strip-piecing adventure. There's little waste. You don't have to worry about matching. It hides boo-boos such as misalignments at the seams. These virtues make it perfect for interjecting either a sliver of contrast or a temperate pause. Allovers adapt to countless moods and behaviors.

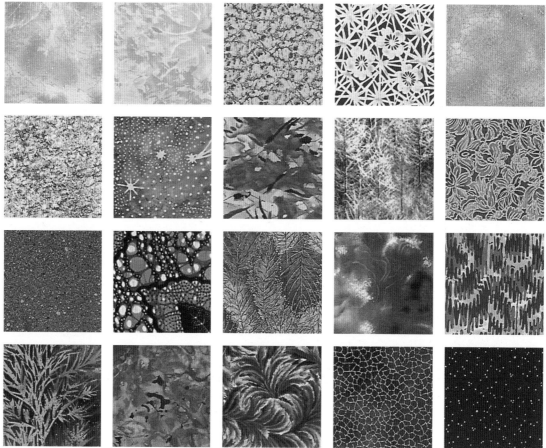

Allover
nondirectional
patterns

We don't usually notice the layout of allovers. The typical allover contains more figure than ground, and at first glance or viewed from a distance may even appear as a solid. (Just so you know, I never use true solids. They function like visual periods, arresting and halting the action. Allovers keep the design moving.) An alternate set spaces the motifs more widely apart, exposing lots of background. A third and very useful set combines both. In one area the design is sparse and loosely packed, then a few inches over it crams together in a congested crowd. Use this type of fabric randomly.

Piecing snowflakes means promoting the translucent nature of these delicate, quickly disappearing structures every chance you get. Look for fabrics to soften straight sewing lines and convey the blurred, vague edges captured in W. A. Bentley's photomicrographs. I love to collect allovers rendered with a painterly, three-dimensional quality. They convey the illusion of substance and help evoke the crystalline quality of a snowflake. The current abundance of dyed, painted, and marbled fabrics is a gold mine of sources for shading and transparency. Borrow shadows and highlights from these fabrics to suggest shifting light falling across the snowflake. When you're foraging for a shadowy effect, play this Leonard Cohen lyric in your head: "There is a crack, a crack in everything. That's how the light gets in." These words suggest patterns that splinter and crackle, as if fissures had shattered the surface, prints that hint at nooks and crannies filled with light and dark. Let the fabric give a few clues, and the audience will fill in the rest.

Fabrics printed with lots of colors in a tiny area energize the most disheartened design. Think dots. I like when dots go bonkers, splattering into colored patterns of randomly tossed speckles, like confetti. Dots organized in a sequential pattern cause the viewer's eye to play connect-the-dots, sparking a dynamic quality.

Dots

Use a variety of big and small allover prints, including textures, gradations, stripes, marbled designs, and stuff speckled with silver. Look for prints on a ground similar in color to the quilt's background. I buy $1/2$- to 1-yard cuts. I continue to be seduced by the novelty of new prints and want to buy them all.

Detail from Snowflake B (page 105)

Snowflake on #266-Indigo by Cherrywood

and on Fossil Fern #528-53 by Benartex.

COMMON GROUND

To establish the illusion of a lacy three-dimensional snowflake, you need to set up a clear distinction between object and background. The various background patches must automatically combine into one continuous negative space. The success of this effect hinges on the background fabric you choose.

Pick a fabric that reads like a solid but isn't a solid. Choose one you really like because you're going to need plenty. I use ½ to ¾ yard of background fabric per snowflake. This amount doesn't include the additional background needed to fit the blocks into a quilt. Make sure the design is nondirectional so that it makes no difference which way it ends up when strip-pieced. Don't be seduced by a directional or set layout no matter how much it begs. If you're not sure, here's the litmus test. Fold the fabric so that it lands on itself randomly. Inspect this juncture and imagine it is a seam. Does it seem seamless, or does it butt itself in an awkward disjointed collision? Keep it simple. You have enough on your mind without having to coach the background into playing its role.

A pure, vibrant, dark color will coax the hues in the fabrics into displaying their own true sensations. I advocate rich luxurious indigo, found on the visual spectrum between blue and violet. Since the fabrics in the snowflake will be a mix of dark, light, and middle values, there will be areas of sharp distinction against the background and areas of soft, melting transitions. Patterns printed on a ground similar to the background fabric will float (or leap, depending on the value contrast) off the surface, and the ground colors will recede into communal negative space. This is how you maneuver the background in and out of frosty nooks and crannies to emphasize the crystal's lacy intricacy or suggest the blurred, soft edges of transition.

In 1992, the background I selected for *Kaleidoscopic XI: Snowfall* was a dyed cotton fabric known for its suedelike appearance and sensuous feel. Seven years later, I opted for a moodier fabric saturated with shadow and dimension. Ten colors interact in this colorway labeled indigo-navy. Both are shown here backing the same snowflake. I like both effects very much. Snowflake A (page 103) shows a third option, an indigo peppered with white.

BLUE AND WHITE

In an indigo-dominated palette, ikats, yukatas, and poplin batiks are ready participants. Ikat is a Malay term accepted worldwide for the process called Kasuri in Japanese. The traditional Japanese form, indigo blue and white on cotton, has been woven for about 150 to 200 years. Yukatas are bold patterns used for unlined, informal summer kimonos. These fabrics can be manipulated to visually connect to the quilt's background fabric, setting up dramatic relationships between the positive shapes and the empty negative ground. Just cut out the patch so that the background color lands at the seamline.

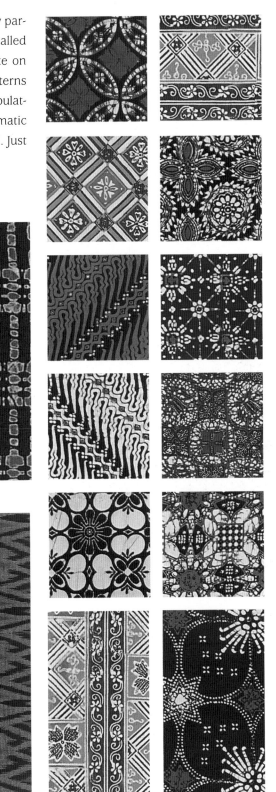

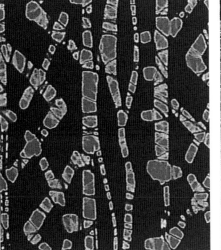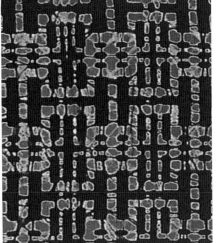

Yukatas

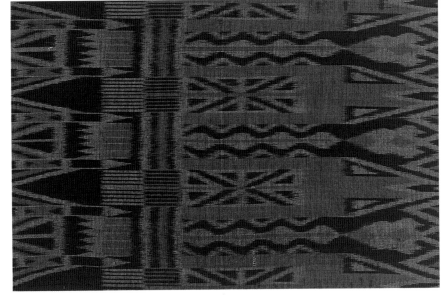

Ikat

Blue and white poplin batiks

CLEVER FABRIC TRICKS

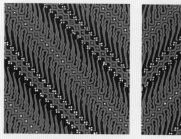

Two-faced batik

Sensuous silk

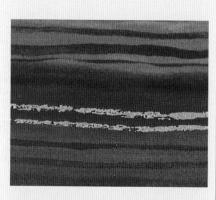

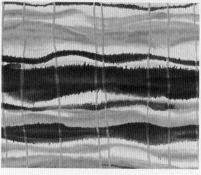

Stripes

The Two-Faced Batik

Part of a batik's appeal is its relaxed, handmade look. That the design is slightly askew makes it even more striking and interesting. Clearly, we would not expect reliable mirror images from these exotic, primitive motifs. Surprise! Batiks are reversible! Because of the dye process, the figures are often equally legible on both sides of the fabric. Usually, you can't tell the right from the wrong side, making batiks an incredibly convenient source for pairs of mirror image motifs. The sometimes slight color shift between the designated front and back can usually be ignored.

The Sensuous Silk

I know it sounds wicked, but I turn my silk into cotton with fusible woven interfacing. This light support stabilizes the silk. Once the silk has been relieved of its free-flowing drape, it strip-pieces like a crisp cotton. Search in fabric shops geared to apparel makers for the flimsiest, most featherweight fusible available (see Sources). If you hand-quilt, test how the interfacing needles. Some adhesives strip the thread or impede the needle's piercing action.

The Versatile Stripe

Think of a striped layout as bands of color stripped together. In a patch intended to be two pieced-together fabrics, substitute a stripe to create the effect of a narrow strip without a bulky seam. Just mark a line on the template where you'd like the stripe to fall, then position the template on the striped fabric. The line imitates a seamline, but in this case, it represents the demarcation between two color bands. Use the template to cut out six patches in each direction. You can use this technique to work in conspicuous jabs of color, soft mellow lines, or even subtle curves.

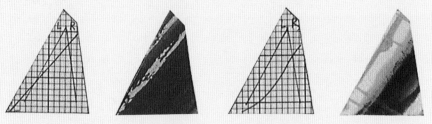

The Artistic License

When it comes to making a quilt, deviating from traditional practices to achieve a certain effect isn't cheating—it's innovative. Use a permanent pen to conceal a misguided color. Appliqué a patch to muffle an overpowering element. Embroider a few stitches to achieve a more graceful transition.

DESIGN CONSIDERATIONS

THE ELEMENTS
Volume

Although a snow crystal is exceedingly thin, often not thicker than heavy paper, it is still a three-dimensional shape defined by its outer edges. Fabricating this delicate sculpture on the flat surface of a quilt means simulating the illusion of a dimensional object viewed from multiple perspectives. On a flat surface, nuances of dark and light impart this three-dimensional quality. Fabrics printed with dramatic shadings and transparencies cause value patterns to spontaneously generate. Areas of high contrast move forward and appear closer while areas of lesser contrast recede, suggesting distance. Multiple values in between suggest the depth between the closest and furthest points.

Radial Balance

That nature opts to manufacture its tiny miracles in recognizable geometric form is part of the snowflake mystique. Snowflakes and hexagons are practically synonymous, so any way we accentuate the six-sided physique promotes instant subject recognition. Within its classic hexagonal form, a snowflake functions like a radial design because all the elements develop symmetrically around a common central point. A radial design directs the viewer's attention into the important center, the primary focal point. The eye travels around the design, making connections between recurring motifs and searching for secondary focal points and accents. Eventually the viewer's attention is drawn back to the center.

That said, this doesn't mean you want a snowflake to look circular. Edit out voluptuous curves and arcs, for this is where snowflake and kaleidoscope designs part ways. A snowflake is rectilinear, meaning its internal forms have straight edges. Emphasize its linear nature by sticking to shapes defined by straight lines. A line parallel to the outer skeletal edge of the hexagon becomes a visual clue and since our eyes tend to follow a line, we trail this one as it bends around the hexagon, forming a smaller hexagon within.

Light & Shadow

W. A. Bentley's photo-taking technique rendered strong contrast between light and shadow. Suggesting light and shadow demands the same design considerations in a quilt as on any two-dimensional canvas. Keep in mind that, in nature, light hits a three-dimensional object at different angles from its differing sides, especially when an irregular light source casts a shadow. The consequence is not simply light and dark, but many variations in between.

Motion

In our role as snowflake makers, we are concerned with two kinds of movement. The first is a visual sensation caused by the movement of the viewer's eye. Luckily for us, radial balance automatically activates this design element by establishing a rhythm based on recurring motifs. The repetitive flow of shapes and color carries the design across the seamlines from wedge to wedge. As the eye moves around, elements reappear in a regular and eventually anticipated order.

The second kind of motion to consider is a physical impression of change—not a manic sensation of speed but rather a slow evaporation. This is motion not through space but through time. As parts of the snowflake alter from a solid to a liquid state, outlines lose their distinctive edge and blur, especially along the periphery. Edges and extremities, instead of being clearly defined, dissolve into incomplete contours. Choose allover fabrics that set up these ambiguous relationships with the background fabric. Although most allovers typically contain more figure than ground, look for ones with lots of ground color showing through and a smattering of pattern on top. Use them randomly so that sometimes there is more background, sometimes more of the fabric's motif, displayed in the patch, making it seem as though the perimeter is not solid but melting at different rates. The pattern will leap forward and appear to float.

Figure & Ground

To "read" a pieced snowflake, the viewer must be able to distinguish between the positive and negative shapes. The snowflake may be the subject and focal point of the composition, but equally important is the way the empty space is organized around it. Some of the most beautiful snowflakes have the most negative space. You don't have to actively design the ground but do be aware that all of the fabrics' backgrounds will merge and reemerge as negative space. There are two categories of backgrounds to consider: (1) your designated reads-like-a-solid background fabric and (2) the dark backdrops of every printed fabric in the patchwork.

To set up this relationship, pick a color for the background fabric that blends with the range of dark blue hues in your stash. You want motifs to advance and backgrounds to connect seamlessly. You need lots of background, so don't pick it as an afterthought. A good background fabric deports itself like an egoless, well-trained butler, receding into the quiet spaces until needed to step forward and offer unobtrusive support.

Degrees of Contrast

Every time I hunt for the next fabric, the search is based on the relationship I want to establish with the previous one. Because of our limited palette, the options will be how light or dark a blue or silver to use. Sometimes I'm looking to continue the mood and want the mild, subtle effect provided by minimal contrast. Other times, I want to clearly define where one pieced unit ends and another begins. That's when I opt for high contrast from fabric to fabric. An area of high contrast creates a line. I find terms like sharp or harsh, mild or minimal useful to define degrees of contrast. I use this vocabulary to focus my options and direct the search.

Multiplicity

The whole is greater than the sum of the parts. What you see in one single triangle is not what you get in the multiplied sum. There is an air of abracadabra as the last seam is stitched because effects more wonderful than you imagined occur. It's hard to believe if you haven't witnessed the magic firsthand. You get to be both the one who makes the magic and the one who is surprised.

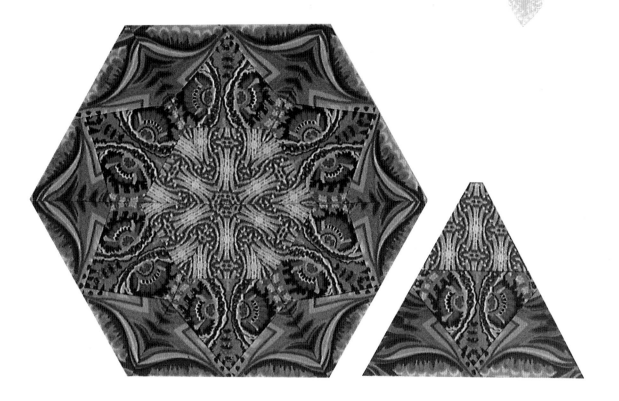

THE PROCESS

Now and then, a design idea simply materializes out of the blue, so to speak. But most of the time, I don't wait for inspiration. I flirt with it, wheedle it, stalk it. I want my quilt to look seamless, but putting it together is not a seamless process. Designing moves forward (and back) in fits and starts. Sometimes I think the magic won't work. Usually, I obsessively stay in that place and try to force it. I whine, I moan, I kvetch, I curse. At times like this, if I can stop feeling depressed because I haven't figured out the big picture and get myself to focus on one small task like marking or cutting, the act of doing something calms me down and moves me one baby step closer to the finish line.

Making a quilt involves so many different tasks, it makes sense to pick one that fits your prevailing mood. Design when your powers of observation are at their most acute, not when something else in your life is vying for attention. Try not to judge how you are doing by how long it takes. I know this is hard because in our complicated lives, time is a premium commodity. Even free time gets rigidly scheduled, making us feel rotten if we can't zoom full speed into the creative zone. The time spent developing an idea differs from problem to problem, and person to person. Keep in mind that when I start a snowflake, I don't relearn the techniques I've just spent ninety-plus pages explaining. And even though I know what I'm doing, I don't complete an intricate block in a day. It's more like four or five long days.

Why are quilters always asked "How long did it take?" Is there a right answer? Is shorter better? Does it make you more clever that you figured out how to race through the process in record time and now you can get on with life's so-called important stuff? Or is longer better because it shows you are industrious and persevering? After examining my labor-intensive quilts, people often say, "My, you have so much patience." Are they suggesting that anyone with stamina and an unusual capacity to cope with boredom could create something like it if they were so inclined? What about skill, artistry, passion? Without comparing myself to Michelangelo, I wonder if that's the first thing they would have said watching him flat on his back for four years.

I'm often asked, what do I do when I don't like the finished version, since I don't do a mock-up. Here's the answer: I critique, audition, whack off, and add more. On a single piece-of-the-pie, I put a scrap of fabric on top of the component that seems out of sync and use mirrors to reflect the impact of the revised version. Typically, this ritual gets repeated with a wide range of fabric snippets before I commit to rehabilitative surgery. Sometimes I decide to leave well enough alone.

Eventually you have to trust the process. At some point I realize an ending is forming, flickering straight ahead like the light at the end of a tunnel, and I make my way toward it with confidence. Sometimes, at this point, I even slow the process down and savor the moment.

PART 3
THE WORKBOOK

Use this workbook as a dry run. Rehearse the process with my fabric choices before setting off on your own.

 SNOWFLAKE A

The Palette

Patches 1 and 2

1. Draw patches 1 and 2 on the diagram. Both patches will be cut from prima donna fabrics.

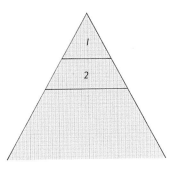

2. Make individual templates for patches 1 and 2, adding ¹⁄₄" seam allowance.

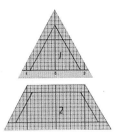

3. Trim the tip of template 1 to ¹⁄₄" (see page 32). Trim the bottom corners of template 1 to match template 2. Mark both templates with fabric hints.

4. Cut six each of patches 1 and 2.

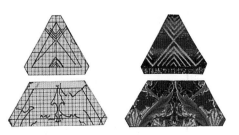

5. Sew six patch (1 + 2)s and set aside.

Make 6

Patches 3, 4, and 5

1. Draw extensions and patches 3, 4, and 5 on the diagram. Patches 3, 4, and 5 will be cut from prima donna fabrics. (The extensions will be added later.)

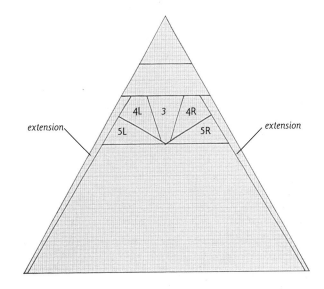

2. Make individual templates for patches 3, 4, and 5, adding ¹⁄₄" seam allowance.

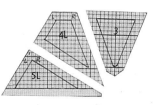

3. Trim the corners of templates 3, 4, and 5 so they match for precision piecing (see Example V, page 56). Mark all three templates with fabric hints.

4. Cut six patch 3s. Cut six left and six right patch 4s. Cut six left and six right patch 5s.

5. Sew six patch (3 + 4L + 5L)s. Sew six patch (4R + 5R)s. Join patches (3·4L·5L) + (4R·5R) to make six patch (3·4·5)s.

Make 6

Patches 6 and 7

1. Draw a center axis (shown here as a blue dashed line) and patches 6 and 7 on the diagram. Patch 6 is a prima donna, and patch 7 is the allover background fabric.

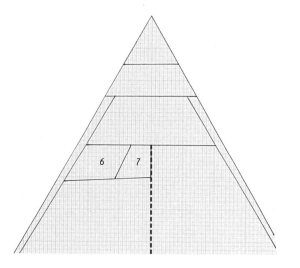

2. Make one template for patch 6 and another template for patch (6 + 7), adding ¼" seam allowance. Template (6 + 7) is used for strip piecing.

3. Mark both template 6s with fabric hints.

4. Cut six left and six right patch 6s.

Patch 6L

5. Strip-piece background fabric to the twelve patch 6s. Use template (6 + 7) to mark the fabric.

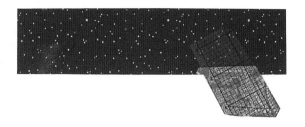

6. Repeat to mark and cut six left and six right patch (6·7)s.

Make 12 (6L and 6R)

Patches 8–18

1. Draw patches 8–18 on the diagram. Patches 8, 12, and 15 are prima donna fabrics. Patch 10 is a directional stripe that can be stripped on. Patch 13 is an allover fabric. Patches 9, 11, 14, 16, 17, and 18 are background fabric.

2. Make a template for patch 8. Cut six left and six right patch 8s.

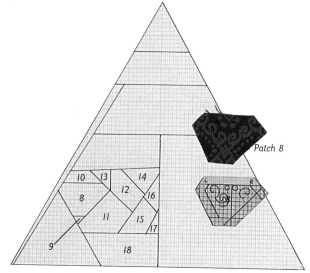

Patch 8

3. Make a template for patch (8 + 9 + 10). Use this template for steps 4 and 5.

4. Strip background fabric 9 to the twelve patch 8s. Cut six left and six right patch (8·9)s.

5. Strip fabric 10 to the twelve patch (8·9)s. Use template (8 + 9 + 10) to cut six left and six right patch (8··10)s.

6. Make a template for patch (8 + 9 + 10 + 11). Strip background fabric to the twelve patch (8··10)s. Use template (8 + 9 + 10 + 11) to cut six left and six right patch (8··11)s.

7. Make one template for patch 12 and another template for patch (12 + 13).

8. Cut six left and six right patch 12s. Strip fabric 13 to the twelve patch 12s. Cut six left and six right patch (12·13)s.

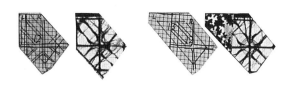

9. Make a template for patch (12 + 13 + 14). Trim corners to match template (8 + 9 + 10 + 11). Strip background fabric to the twelve patch (12·13)s. Use template (12 + 13 + 14) to cut six left and six right patch (12··14)s.

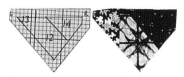

10. Join patches (8··11) + (12··14) to make twelve patch (8··14)s.

11. Make one template for patch 15 and another template for patch (15 + 16).

12. Cut six left and six right patch 15s. Strip background fabric to the twelve patch 15s. Use the template to cut six left and six right patch (15·16)s.

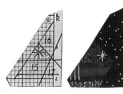

13. Make a template for patch (15 + 16 + 17). Strip background fabric to the twelve patch (15·16)s. Use the template to cut six left and six right patch (15··17)s.

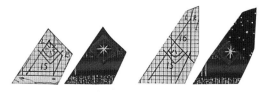

14. Join patches (8··14) + (15··17) to make twelve patch (8··17)s.

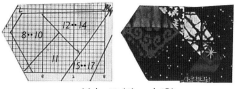
Make 12 (6L and 6R)

15. Make template (8 + 9 + 10 + 11 + 12 + 13 + 14 + 15 + 16 + 17 + 18) Strip background fabric to the twelve patch (8··17)s. Use template to cut six left and six right patch (8··18)s.

16. Join patches (6·7) + (8··18) to make twelve patch (6··18)s.

Patches 19–26

1. Draw patches 19–26 on the diagram. Patch 25 is a prima donna. Patches 19, 21, and 23 are allovers (19 and 21 are the same fabric). Patches 20, 22, 24, and 26 are background fabric. In this section, the inner unit is strip-pieced, starting from one end. An alternate approach is to start at the middle and add on in both directions (see Example IV, page 52).

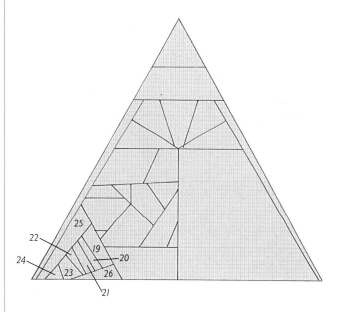

2. Make a template for patch (19 + 20). Strip fabric 19 to background fabric. Cut six left and six right patch (19·20)s.

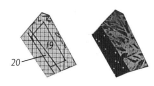

3. Make a template for patch (19 + 20 + 21). Strip fabric 21 to the twelve patch (19·20)s. Use the template to cut six left and six right patch (19··21)s.

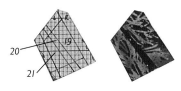

4. Make a template for patch (19 + 20 + 21 + 22). Strip background fabric to the twelve patch (19··21)s. Use the template to cut six left and six right patch (19··22)s.

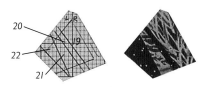

5. Make a template for patch (19 + 20 + 21 + 22 + 23). Strip fabric 23 to the twelve patch (19··22)s. Use the template to cut six left and six right patch (19··23)s.

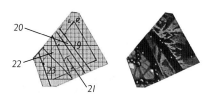

6. Make a template for patch (19 + 20 + 21 + 22 + 23 + 24). Strip background fabric to the twelve patch (19··23)s. Use the template to cut six left and six right patch (19··24)s.

7. Make a template for patch 25. Trim corners to match template (19 + 20 + 21 + 22 + 23 + 24). Cut six left and six right patch 25s. Join patches 25 + (19··24) to make twelve patch (19··25)s.

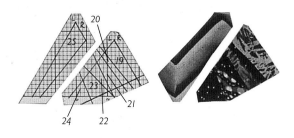

8. Make a template for patch (19 + 20 + 21 + 22 + 23 + 24 + 25 + 26). Strip background fabric to the twelve patch (19··25)s. Use the template to cut six left and six right patch (19··26)s.

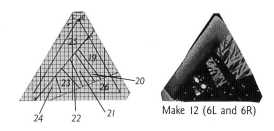

Make 12 (6L and 6R)

Here's the reason I chose to add the patch 25 prima donna fabric before the patch 26 background fabric: Adding on a prima donna patch is always a gamble. Odds are one of the twelve will be a little askew. Adding an allover last provides an opportunity to even out any discrepancies.

9. Join patches (6·18) + (19·26) to make six left and six right patch (6··26)s.

10. Sew the left and right patch (6··26)s together in pairs along the center axis to make six units.

11. Join each unit (6··26) to a patch (3·4·5) to make six (3··26) units.

Patch 27—Side Extensions

1. Referring to the finished diagram, make a template for entire wedge except patches 1 and 2; add 1/4" seam allowance. Strip on the extensions to each (3··26) unit. Use the template to cut six wedge bottoms.

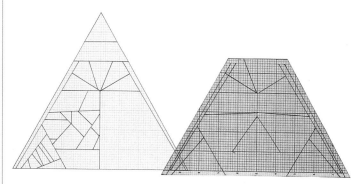

2. Join each wedge bottom to a patch (1·2) to create six individual 60° wedges.

Make 6

All Together Now

Sew the six 60° wedges into the hexagon.

Close your eyes. When you open them, see what catches your eye first. Probably the all-important center.

The motifs in patches 3, 5, 8, and 15 float off the flat surface because the ground color in these fabrics connects visually to the background fabric. Patch 15 is particularly effective. The star pops but doesn't take over, coaching the viewer's eye around the hexagon from wedge to wedge. The ombré stripe adds complexity, setting off a vibration that is really cool. Because the transition from one band of color to another is soft and subtle, the vague, blurred edge of the important royal blue striation is perfect. Patch 25 is another example of an ombré. It's used effectively to draw the viewer's attention to the tips of the extensions and organize the branching forms.

The combination of the left- and right-sided patch 5 creates a pleasing curve that convincingly erases the seams between it and patch 6. Although curves aren't typically cast as a snowflake form, these lovely motifs seem sincere and are not overpowering.

Find the connection between patch 2 and the extensions. The low contrast between these fabrics sets up a continuous relationship. Patch 6 also seems to grow out of the extension because, once again, the value contrast between the two fabrics is minimal. This, in turn, causes the graceful motif in patch 5 to connect to both patch 6 and the extension.

Find patches 13, 19, and 23. Because these versatile allover fabrics are denser in some areas than others, they soften the straight sewing seams and convey the indistinct edges suggested in photomicrographs. This background, peppered with a tiny dot, is different from any other example in this book. Here's your chance to see if you like this effect.

SNOWFLAKE B
from *Kaleidoscopic XXII: Ice Crystals*

a.

b.

c.

d.

a. *The Palette*

b. *The Diagram*

c. *The Bentley Photomicrograph*

d. *The Wedge*

e. *The Pieced Snowflake*

e.

SNOWFLAKE C
from *Kaleidoscopic XXII: Ice Crystals*

a.

b.

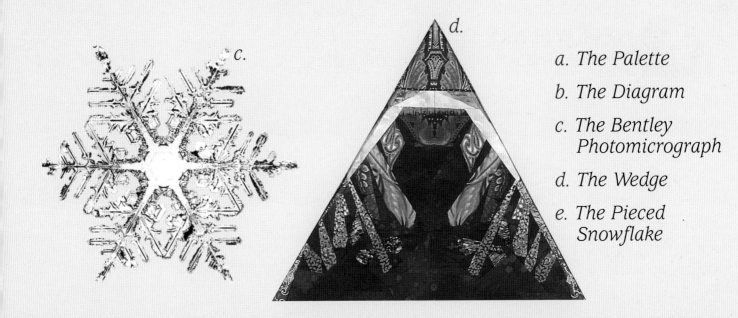

c.

d.

a. *The Palette*

b. *The Diagram*

c. *The Bentley Photomicrograph*

d. *The Wedge*

e. *The Pieced Snowflake*

SNOWFLAKE D
from *Kaleidoscopic XXII: Ice Crystals*

a.

b.

c.

a. *The Diagram*

b. *The Bentley Photomicrograph*

c. *The Wedge*

d. *The Pieced Snowflake*

INDEX

SOURCES

Wilson Alwyn Bentley

The "Snowflake" Bentley Exhibit
The Jericho Historical Society
The Old Red Mill
P. O. Box 35
Jericho, VT 05465
(802) 899-3225
www.snowflakebentley.com
(official Bentley website)

*The Wilson Bentley
Digital Archives (Volume I)*
CD-ROM containing over 1,000
snowflake images, frost, dew, and other
photography, articles written by Bentley,
other documents, a film clip of the man
at his camera (circa 1917), and more.
(802) 899-1739
snowbliz@aol.com
www.snowflakebentley.com

Snow Crystals
by W. A. Bentley and W. J Humphreys
(20287-9)
Dover Publications, Inc.
Dept. 23, 31 East 2nd Street
Mineola, NY 11501
Write for free catalog.
This book is also available through the
Jericho Historical Society (see above).

Snowflake Bentley
by Jacqueline Briggs Martin
Illustrated by Mary Azarian
Houghton Mifflin Co, 1998
Illustrated children's book, winner
of The Caldecott Medal
This book is available through the
Jericho Historical Society (see above).

Fabrics by Paula Nadelstern

Bernartex
1460 Broadway, Dept PN
New York, NY 10036
Http://www.benartex.com
Inquire about "Symmetry"
and "Serendipity."

The Cotton Club
P. O. Box 2263
Boise, ID 83701
(208) 345-5567, fax (208) 345-1217
cotton@micron.net
http://www.cottonclub.com
Mail-order source for Paula's fabrics,
notecards and wrapping paper, prints
with repetitive/symmetrical motifs, large
protractors with easy-to-read numbers,
see-thru template material, rulers and
graph paper pads with eight-to-the-inch-
grid, and more.

Other Fabrics

Cherrywood Fabrics
P. O. Box 486
Brainerd, MN 56401
(888) 298-0967
Hand-dyed suede look cotton

Handloom Batik
Att: Usha
214 Mulberry Street
New York, NY 10012
(212) 925-9542
Source for blue and white 100%
cotton poplin batiks (page 91).
Send SASE for information.

International Fabric Collection
3445 West Lake Road
Erie, PA 16505-3661
(800) 462-3891
Liberty of London tana lawn;
fusible interfacing.

Niu Imports
P. O. Box 428
Laie, HI 96762
(808) 293-9819
66EYT Yukata Fabric,
approximately $13 per meter.

Skydyes
Mickey Lawler
83 Richmond Lane
West Hartford, CT 06117
Write for price list of
hand-painted fabric.

Thai Silks
252 State Street
Los Altos, CA 94022
(800) 722-SILK

Quilt Photography

Karen Bell
139 West 19th Street #1C
New York, NY 10011
Send SASE for rate sheet.

John Wooden
415 South 47th Street
Philadelphia, PA 19143
Send SASE for rate sheet.

Products

The Brooklyn Revolver
Come Quilt With Me
3903 Avenue I
Brooklyn, NY 11210
Phone or fax (718) 377-3652
Circular rotary mat mounted
on a lazy Susan.

Dick Blick Art Materials
(800) 447-8192
info@dickblick.com
Pens, see-through rulers,
graph paper, art supplies.

Displayaway
(888) ITS-SAFE (487-7233)
Zellerwood@aol.com
This clever, safe, attractive display
system allows quilts to be hung
and removed in minutes.

Steinlauf & Stoller, Inc.
239 West 39th Street
New York, NY 10018
Toll-free: (877) 869-0321
(212) 869-0321, 869-0322;
fax: (212) 302-4465
www.steinlaufandstoller.com
Distributors of notions including
featherweight fusible interfacing
(CL-FW) $30.00 minimum

ABOUT THE AUTHOR

Paula Nadelstern travels extensively teaching her unique kaleidoscopic quilt-making techniques. Her award-winning quilts have been featured internationally in exhibits, including a solo exhibit mounted at The Museum of the American Quilters Society, on television shows and online websites, and in books and magazines. Recently, one of her quilts was included in the "Twentieth Century's 100 Best American Quilts" exhibit. A recipient of Artists' Fellowships from the New York Foundation for the Arts and The Bronx Council on the Arts, Paula currently designs textile prints exclusively for Benartex, Inc.

Photo by Jim Whitaker

Another book by Paula Nadelstern

KALEIDOSCOPES & QUILTS

PAULA NADELSTERN

For more information about other C&T titles write for a free catalog:
C&T Publishing, Inc.
P.O Box 1456
Lafayette, CA 94549
(800) 284-1114
e-mail: ctinfo@ctpub.com
website: www.ctpub.com

For quilting supplies:
Cotton Patch Mail Order
3405 Hall Lane,
Dept. CTB
Lafayette, CA 94549
(800) 835-4418
(925) 283-7883
e-mail: quiltusa@yahoo.com
website: www.quiltusa.com